84p
2

D0309827

Stilus Artifex

STILUS ARTIFEX

by C. Stace and P. V. Jones

Cambridge at the University Press
1972

Published by the Syndics of the Cambridge University Press
Bentley House, 200 Euston Road, London NW1 2DB
American Branch: 32 East 57th Street, New York, N.Y.10022

© Cambridge University Press 1972

Library of Congress Catalogue Card Number: 78–164453

ISBN: 0 521 08143 2

Printed in Great Britain
at the University Printing House, Cambridge
(Brooke Crutchley, University Printer)

FRANCIS HOLLAND.
CHURCH OF ENGLAND SCHOOL
LIBRARY
870·9 STA
72·370
57 c

CONTENTS

ACKNOWLEDGEMENTS

For permission to include copyright material acknowledgement is made to the following:

Penguin Books Ltd. for quotations from A. E. Watt's translation of *Propertius*, E. V. Rieu's translation of the *Odyssey* and E. F. Watling's translation of *Sophocles' Oedipus Coloneus* in *The Theban Plays*; the Clarendon Press for a quotation from R. Syme's *The Roman Revolution* and from W. J. Cory's translation of *Callimachus* included in *The Oxford Book of Greek Verse in Translation*; Routledge and Kegan Paul Ltd. and Humanities Press, Inc., for a quotation from a translation in K. Quinn's *Latin Explorations*; L. P. Wilkinson for quotations from translations in *Ovid Recalled*, published by Cambridge University Press; The New American Library, Inc., New York for a quotation from Patric Dickinson's translation of the *Aeneid*; University of Chicago Press for a quotation from Richmond Lattimore's translation of the *Odes of Pindar*. A quotation from *Sophocles' Oedipus at Colonus* translated by Robert Fitzgerald, copyright 1941, by Harcourt Brace Jovanovich, Inc.; renewed 1969, by Robert Fitzgerald, is reprinted by permission of the publishers.

INTRODUCTION

From the outset, the task of literary criticism is beset with difficulties. Indeed the question of the possibility of teaching such a procedure is often challenged. When one is dealing with dead, foreign languages, which are often different in style, spirit and thought from our own, removed from our own age by two thousand years or more of change, it is hardly even to be hoped that we can entirely appreciate the true feeling, style or even the sense of some of that literature, let alone the point of every reference, every nuance, in the way that an intelligent Roman or Greek would have done. But that is the desideratum. It is a forlorn undertaking; but there are degrees of unsuccess.

Plainly much has to be done by trial and error. At best the exercise may be a compromise, at worst a thoroughly subjective statement of one person's – possibly lunatic – views. But better a subjective appreciation than none at all.

The difficulties of teaching an aesthetic approach will be plain to all who have tried; plain, too, to those who have read some of the recent spate of critical works on the Classics. Aesthetics are so much a personal matter. There are no laws to dictate what a pupil may, or may not, see, hear or read into a line. But this is not to say that one may not *direct* the gaze of a pupil, in the hope that he may be trained by experience to understand what a writer intended, and by experience to evaluate this. The questions in this book are intended to give such direction. They do not pretend to point to one correct answer – indeed, by no means all of the questions *have* one particular answer, and it should be made clear that we have often asked questions which we thought needed to be asked, but to which we ourselves claim to have no clear-cut 'answer'. The questions may serve as a basis for the kind of discussion which helps to arrive at a reasonable conclusion.

Again, we are faced with a serious problem when we try to decide exactly what we need to know about an author and his background in order successfully to evaluate a passage. Is it possible, for example, to enjoy a sensible appreciation of Aristophanes or Juvenal without a knowledge of the social conditions in which they lived? Will Virgil be understood if we have no knowledge of the meaning of the Augustan age to the Romans, or if we are unaware of the literary tradition within which he worked? While most sensitive critics will realise the artistic greatness of Homer without a deep knowledge of the basically oral tradition within which he composed, how satisfying can our evaluation of the whole scope of his work be without some sort of background knowledge of this kind? At the deepest level, of course, we cannot fully appreciate an author if we know nothing of his life, or social and literary background. Yet this question both poses and answers the problem for a book of this scale; we must presume that the teacher and his pupils are 'sensitive people'. And again, we are not asking the pupil to evaluate the whole scope of a work, but carefully selected extracts and examples, which seem to us to be of merit, and in so far as this is possible, to be comprehensible in themselves. If the teacher feels a need to impart to his pupils a knowledge of an author's background (and we trust that he will), then let him do so using his own understanding and experience, and so encourage the pupil, by showing his own interest in areas of knowledge not strictly covered by the questions appended to the text, to try to see the part clearly by grasping the whole.

Such appraisal, of course, depends on the eye and the ear – indeed the very temperament and personality of the critic; a criticism is, of its nature, subjective. But it may become, by practice, a more balanced criticism, less idiosyncratic than it might have been. To expect every pupil, however, to become a brilliant and perceptive critic as a result of this approach may be fanciful, but in the light of past experiment we feel quite confident that the average pupil will benefit.

The crucial problem is the choice of level at which one may pitch a question in order to have a reasonable chance of obtaining a response, and it is on this that the ultimate success of critical exercises depends. *Aestimanda*, by M. G. Balme and M. S. Warman of Harrow School (OUP 1965), has proved beyond doubt that such exercises can be a successful means of strengthening the 'critical muscles'. This excellent book has elicited a response from our pupils which has frankly surpassed all our expectations, and thereby provided the encouragement for the experiment to be tried again. With university scholarship examinations becoming more and more biased towards testing a pupil's power of literary judgement, textbooks of the *Aestimanda* type must and will be increasingly forthcoming.

The challenge has been taken up by two other books of similar kind: *Aere Perennius* by D. G. Fratter (1968) and *Reading Latin Poetry* by R. Hornsby (1967). For details of these see the Bibliography at the end of this book. For various reasons we have found both of these books to be less satisfactory than *Aestimanda*.

In the main, *Aestimanda* used three types of exercises:

(*a*) The 'analytical' type (a passage followed by analytical questions), which formed 45% of the total (27% in *Aere Perennius*).

(*b*) The comparison of passages of similar theme or purpose (29%: 55% in *A.P.*).

(*c*) The evaluation of different translations of a passage (16%: 7% in *A.P.*).

We feel that this kind of emphasis is the correct one. Our own bias, therefore, is towards the analytical type of exercise (*a*). There is also a number of thematic exercises (*b*) (especially in Part four), so that the student can try to see the idea as a whole within Classical literature, and relate it, wherever possible, to the literature of his own and other languages. Comparison should be, after all, a means of widening the perspective. Plainly, passages given for such comparison must usually bear a close affinity to each other, although we do not rule out the possibility that it is occasionally good for a pupil to point out exactly why and how two passages are *dis*similar.

The third of our main groups of exercises – (*c*) the comparison of versions of a given original – is the smallest. This method of eliciting criticism has been under some question, but does offer the pupil variety, and, at best, may direct his critical attention to the original in a concentrated way, and thus perhaps improve his grasp of the language, and the quality of his own translation.

Other types of exercise are included in small numbers. The type of exercise where a pupil is asked to assign a passage to its author has been used very sparingly, this being, in our own experience at least, an operation too sophisticated for the average pupil, except where questions of a very pointed nature are appended, or where such passages – of the best known authors – are presented in such a way as to make their stylistic point with the utmost clarity.

Our aim is that of our predecessors: to promote the appreciation of Classical literature by exercising the student in the interpretation and critical evaluation of selections from some of the best that Classical literature has to offer. We have endeavoured to give this book the widest possible scope by confining it neither to Latin, nor to verse, in the hope that prose and verse in both languages may be accorded the same critical approach. As a general rule we have avoided passages dealt with by *Aestimanda* and *Aere Perennius*, although a small amount of overlap has proved inevitable; in such cases the passages used are either put to different purposes, or the questions slanted in a different way. Our ultimate aim is clear: that pupils will transfer the critical attitude encouraged by these exercises to every piece of Classical literature they meet, and submit it to the same analysis and the same process of appraisal.

We have found it convenient to divide the exercises into four parts in order of increasing difficulty. Part one, for example, can be tackled by those in the post 'O' level year, while Part three is intended for second year sixth-formers and above. Part four contains some longer exercises which are often rather more difficult, more time-consuming and more demanding than the exercises in the other three parts.

The questions appended to the texts are not arranged in any set order which we consider to be the 'correct' order. There seems to be no 'correct' order in which questions should be asked. Often, however, we have found it a useful procedure to ask for general impressions first, then to attempt an analysis of the text which is followed by a confirmation or refutation of the first impression. In other exercises, we have tried to lead up to a conclusion by a series of pointed analytical questions, usually beginning with matters of sense and interpretation and

x

moving on to a consideration of emotions, style, attitude etc. There will sometimes be an overlap between questions, and thus it will be wise to deal with some questions orally and to ask for written answers to others. We leave this choice entirely to the teacher's judgement; but it will be obvious that certain types of questions, where they occur, lend themselves more readily than others to class discussion. More difficult questions of a metrical nature are usually relegated to the end of each set of questions, so that they may be omitted where desired. Metrical questions of a general nature will be found throughout, since a pupil must have at least a working knowledge of the principles of versification to enable him to appreciate any kind of poetry.

Sometimes the questions will be angled in such a way as to elicit a particular interpretation – it is impossible in every case both to give help and to appear neutral. We plead that in no case are the interpretations inclined towards either eccentric opinions or the opinions of a small minority.

Although the great majority of the passages selected for criticism are intended to stand on their own, and no special knowledge should be needed to tackle them, we have given brief introductory notes where necessary.

A short glossary of technical terms will be found at the end of the book; this may be useful to the beginner, and serve as an *aide-mémoire* to the more experienced. It includes grammatical and metrical terms, figures of speech etc.

Finally, a brief bibliography of selected critical works has been appended. This is a purely personal choice and does not pretend to be representative of the whole range of critical literature which has recently been published.

We must, and are happy to, acknowledge our debts to various scholars and their works. We have used the now standard works a great deal (see the Bibliography), in particular L. P. Wilkinson's *Golden Latin Artistry*, K. Quinn's *Latin Explorations*, and Volume 1 of *Critical Essays in Roman Literature* (ed. J. P. Sullivan). We would like to endorse the remarks made by the authors of *Aestimanda* about *Golden Latin Artistry*; anything Mr Wilkinson writes is at once scholarly and fascinating. We strongly recommend this book as a *vade mecum* for any pupil who is to attempt our exercises.

We look forward to hearing the criticisms of all who are interested in Classical literature, and express the hope that they will take up the challenge, experiment with our exercises and set to work making their own improvements. Only by a process of trial and error can we hope to produce the books which will be vital to the survival of Classics in the years ahead.

We should like to express our thanks to those who in various ways have helped in the compiling of this book. First, to Mr M. G. Balme and Mr M. S. Warman of Harrow School, for criticism of a kind which only the authors of *Aestimanda* could have given. This was invariably constructive and humbly offered. We owe a great deal to their enthusiasm and encouragement, and are glad publicly to acknowledge it. Secondly, to colleagues who have readily given advice, or used their pupils as guinea-pigs: Mr A. G. Hunt of Fitzwilliam College, Cambridge; Mr J. Picken and Mr N. W. McN. Clark of George Watson's College, Edinburgh; Mr R. H. Philp of Fettes College, Edinburgh; Mr R. A. Morris; Miss G. Murray of St Paul's Girls' School, London; Mr J. A. Williams of The Skinners' Company School, Tunbridge Wells; also to Professors E. W. Handley and O. Skutsch of University College, London, and Professor R. P. Winnington-Ingram of King's College, London, for expert advice of various kinds. Thirdly, to the pupils of Christ's Hospital, who have responded most encouragingly to innumerable 'trial runs', and have played a vital part in the shaping of this book.

Finally, thanks are due to the Staff of the Cambridge University Press for their friendly and skilful advice on every occasion.

C. S.

P. V. J.

1971

ADVICE TO THE READER

What is the essence of literary criticism? How does one set about it? We are aware that our approach to this problem is 'classical', in the sense that it is a well-tried and traditional one. Over the last ten years there have been many new directions taken in the field of literary criticism which have proved of value and significance. Particularly, we must mention the efforts made to see the relationship between linguistic usage and social and cultural background, and between the way we speak and the way we think; also there has been an attempt to be more precise about the ways in which we traditionally express value-judgements about literature and society (see Bibliography). But the wheels of Classical scholarship turn slowly, and it would be out of place in a book such as this to experiment when so little work has been done in relating Classical literature to this kind of approach. We look forward, however, to seeing books which will attempt the synthesis. Meanwhile it is hoped that the exercises themselves may explain what is involved in the task of literary criticism, or at least make it clearer. For the complete tiro, we outline here a general plan of procedure, along traditional lines, as a starting point.

Read the passage through aloud once or twice: Then:

(1) The first step is to discover the *sense* – i.e. to make an accurate translation. (We assume that pupils will have access to the *Oxford Classical Dictionary* – or, e.g., *The Oxford Companion to Classical Literature* – and, in cases of difficulty, to the standard editions of the great Classical authors. A limited amount of linguistic help has been given, especially in Part 1. Elsewhere it is assumed that the text is understood before the questions are attempted.)

(2) Next, *analysis*. Consider, so far as is possible, every emotion and effect the writer was trying to produce. Feeling, tone, intention, attitude, style must be taken into account at this stage. (A definition of such terms may be found on p. xv.)

(3) *Judgement* or *evaluation*. Attempt to evaluate the success of the passage under consideration. Try to put yourself in the writer's place, and assess the validity of what he is saying, and the way it is said. (Poetry, for example, is usually relating and interpreting some kind of experience – assess the truth of this interpretation.) Consider the response which the writing evokes in yourself, and try to account for it.

Literary appreciation depends upon the successful completion of all three of these stages.

DEFINITION OF TERMS USED

The task of literary criticism is made more difficult by vagueness in the use of critical terminology. It is, therefore, best to attempt at the outset to clarify some of the most important terms used rather than to let a pupil assume his own meanings and encounter difficulties later on. The following definitions apply to their usage in this book and are not necessarily of universal validity.

form – the arrangement, mode of construction; the shape and structure which give a piece of writing some of its most essential qualities.

intention – the effect the writer is trying, consciously or unconsciously, to produce.

feeling – the mood or atmosphere of the writing; the writer's attitude towards his subject-matter.

tone – the writer's attitude to his reader/audience, *or* to his subject-matter, as shown by the 'colour', quality and effect of his words and phrases.

attitude – occasionally *viewpoint*; the way in which a writer regards his theme.

theme – the proposition or central idea of which the text is an illustration.

style – the choice and arrangement of words; the way in which the writer chooses to express his thoughts.

There will inevitably be a certain amount of overlapping of these terms, and other terms may from time to time occur. Where these are not considered self-explanatory they should be defined before a class begins.

PART ONE

1 *A heart of oak*

The love-sick Dido has begged her sister Anna to plead with
Aeneas not to leave Carthage. Anna's appeals are in vain:
Aeneas' mind is made up.

> Talibus orabat, talisque miserrima fletus
> fertque refertque soror. sed nullis ille movetur
> fletibus aut voces ullas tractabilis audit;
> fata obstant placidasque viri deus obstruit auris.
> ac velut annoso validam cum robore quercum   5
> Alpini Boreae nunc hinc nunc flatibus illinc
> eruere inter se certant; it stridor, et altae
> consternunt terram concusso stipite frondes;
> ipsa haeret scopulis et quantum vertice ad auras
> aetherias, tantum radice in Tartara tendit: 10
> haud secus adsiduis hinc atque hinc vocibus heros
> tunditur, et magno persentit pectore curas;
> mens immota manet, lacrimae volvuntur inanes.
>
> Virgil, *Aeneid* IV. 437–49

1 Examine this simile in detail and write a critical appreciation of the way in which it is applied. In how many
   respects, and how closely, does Aeneas resemble the oak
   tree described by Virgil? Is the simile effective in all its
   details – or does it fall down anywhere?
2 Explain the meaning of *placidas* (v. 4).
3 There has been much discussion about the tears in v. 13
   (*lacrimae*). To whom do they belong, in your opinion:
   Anna, Dido or Aeneas himself? What meanings would
   inanes take on in each case? How does *mens immota* (v. 13)
   affect your decision and what, in the simile, might affect
   your opinion?
4 What does this short passage imply about the character of
   Aeneas? Does Virgil represent him here as a plaything of

Fate, or rather as a man hardened against persuasion by a sense of personal destiny? Which is more likely to have been Virgil's intention? Does this help your interpretation of v. 13?

5 How is rhythm used effectively in this extract? Give two examples, and explain in detail what effect is produced, and how.

2   The poet's mistress

Quintia formosa est multis. mihi candida, longa,
   recta est: haec ego sic singula confiteor.
totum illud formosa nego: nam nulla venustas,
   nulla in tam magno est corpore mica salis.
Lesbia formosa est, quae cum pulcerrima tota est,   5
   tum omnibus una omnis surripuit Veneres.

Catullus LXXXVI

1 What is the poem concerned with, i.e. what is the central idea?
2 What exactly does v. 6 mean?
3 What does *formosus* mean? What other Latin words are used to describe beauty in love-poetry?
4 What qualities does Catullus decide the ideal woman must possess?
5 Quinn translates *nam nulla venustas* as 'No. She's no charm, no grace.' Do you agree with this interpretation of *venustas*? (Use a dictionary.)

3   A Vestal Virgin is punished

Missi statim pontifices qui defodiendam necandamque curarent. illa nunc ad Vestam, nunc ad ceteros deos manus tendens, multa sed hoc frequentissime clamitabat: 'me Caesar incestam putat, qua sacra faciente vicit triumphavit!' blandiens haec an inridens, ex fiducia sui an ex contemptu 5 principis dixerit, dubium est. dixit donec ad supplicium, nescio an innocens, certe tamquam innocens ducta est. quin

2

etiam cum in illud subterraneum demitteretur, haesissetque
descendenti stola, vertit se ac recollegit, cumque ei manum
carnifex daret, aversata est et resiluit foedumque contactum 10
quasi plane a casto puroque corpore novissima sanctitate
reiecit omnibusque numeris pudoris
                'πολλὴν πρόνοιαν ἔσχεν εὐσχήμων πεσεῖν'.
                              Pliny, *Epistulae* IV. 11 (part)
13. *Tr.* 'She showed a strong solicitude to fall with decency.'

1 'Apart from the fussiness of Pliny's account, it is the
   moralising tone that offends' (Quinn, *Latin Explorations*
   118). Discuss. Do you agree with either of the two
   charges? Illustrate your answer from the text.
2 'There is much too much explanation of motive, too much
   fuss over incidental detail' (Quinn, *ibid.*). Is this a fair
   judgement? How much can we exonerate Pliny from such
   criticisms by saying that it is impossible to create much
   'atmosphere' in a letter to a friend?
3 What impression is Pliny trying to create, and what means
   does he use?

4 *Happy landings*

Odysseus, after twenty years of wandering, is about to be
taken back to Ithaca by his Phaeacian hosts.

Αὐτὰρ ἐπεί ῥ' ἐπὶ νῆα κατήλυθον ἠδὲ θάλασσαν,
αἶψα τά γ' ἐν νηὶ γλαφυρῇ πομπῆες ἀγαυοὶ
δεξάμενοι κατέθεντο, πόσιν καὶ βρῶσιν ἅπασαν·
κὰδ δ' ἄρ' Ὀδυσῆϊ στόρεσαν ῥῆγός τε λίνον τε
νηὸς ἐπ' ἰκριόφιν γλαφυρῆς, ἵνα νήγρετον εὕδοι,   5
πρύμνης· ἂν δὲ καὶ αὐτὸς ἐβήσετο καὶ κατέλεκτο
σιγῇ· τοὶ δὲ καθῖζον ἐπὶ κληῖσιν ἕκαστοι
κόσμῳ, πεῖσμα δ' ἔλυσαν ἀπὸ τρητοῖο λίθοιο.
εὖθ' οἱ ἀνακλινθέντες ἀνερρίπτουν ἅλα πηδῷ,
καὶ τῷ νήδυμος ὕπνος ἐπὶ βλεφάροισιν ἔπιπτε,   10
νήγρετος ἥδιστος, θανάτῳ ἄγχιστα ἐοικώς.
ἡ δ', ὥς τ' ἐν πεδίῳ τετράοροι ἄρσενες ἵπποι,
πάντες ἅμ' ὁρμηθέντες ὑπὸ πληγῇσιν ἱμάσθλης,

3

ὑψόσ' ἀειρόμενοι ῥίμφα πρήσσουσι κέλευθον,
ὡς ἄρα τῆς πρύμνη μὲν ἀείρετο, κῦμα δ' ὄπισθε   15
πορφύρεον μέγα θῦε πολυφλοίσβοιο θαλάσσης.
ἡ δὲ μάλ' ἀσφαλέως θέεν ἔμπεδον · οὐδέ κεν ἴρηξ
κίρκος ὁμαρτήσειεν, ἐλαφρότατος πετεηνῶν.
ὡς ἡ ῥίμφα θέουσα θαλάσσης κύματ' ἔταμνεν,
ἄνδρα φέρουσα θεοῖς ἐναλίγκια μήδε' ἔχοντα,   20
ὃς πρὶν μὲν μάλα πολλὰ πάθ' ἄλγεα ὃν κατὰ θυμὸν
ἀνδρῶν τε πτολέμους ἀλεγεινά τε κύματα πείρων,
δὴ τότε γ' ἀτρέμας εὗδε, λελασμένος ὅσσ' ἐπεπόνθει.

Homer, *Odyssey* XIII. 70–92

1 What sort of contrast does Homer point between Odysseus
   and the sailors, and why?
2 In the simile at vv. 12ff., what is being compared with
   the ship? Is the comparison an exact one?
3 Why does the poet bring in the ἴρηξ at v. 17?
4 How does the feeling alter within vv. 19–23? Consider
   metre, sound and sense.
5 Try to translate vv. 12–19 to catch the same feeling of
   being at sea as the Greek does.

5   *Death of the ox*

At the end of the third *Georgic*, Virgil is describing a pestilence
in Southern Italy which destroyed all the animals in the area.
Having pictured the dying horse, Virgil now turns to the
death of the ox.

Ecce autem duro fumans sub vomere taurus
concidit et mixtum spumis vomit ore cruorem
extremosque ciet gemitus. it tristis arator
maerentem abiungens fraterna morte iuvencum,
atque opere in medio defixa reliquit aratra.   5
non umbrae altorum nemorum, non mollia possunt
prata movere animum, non qui per saxa volutus
purior electro campum petit amnis; at ima
solvuntur latera, atque oculos stupor urget inertis
ad terramque fluit devexo pondere cervix.   10

quid labor aut benefacta iuvant? quid vomere terras
invertisse gravis? atqui non Massica Bacchi
munera, non illis epulae nocuere repostae:
frondibus et victu pascuntur simplicis herbae,
pocula sunt fontes liquidi atque exercita cursu   15
flumina, nec somnos abrumpit cura salubris.

Virgil, Georgics III. 515–30

12. *Massica*: Massicus was a mountain in Campania, at the foot of which
grew the famous Falernian vine.
13. *repostae*: 'replenished' (referring to the various courses which made up
the Roman *cena*).
15. *exercita*: 'driven'.

1 What does Virgil intend the reader to feel about the death
  of the ox?
2 How does the poet use rhythm and sound expressively in
  v. 2?
3 Wilkinson (*Golden Latin Artistry* 197) says of v. 3: 'The
  monosyllabic *it*, coming first in its sentence, focuses the
  eye on the desolate ploughman.' Do you consider this
  interpretation fanciful? If so, what comment would you
  make on the word order and choice of words?
4 Explain the repetition (*non...non...non*) in vv. 5 ff. and
  try to define the feeling of vv. 6–8.
5 What is the effect of the two questions in vv. 11 12? What
  does Virgil have in mind in v. 13 (*non illis* etc.)?
6 Where does the reader receive the clearest impression that
  Virgil considered the ox a noble animal, and its simple life
  a fine life?

6   Nero — near the end

Sed revocato rursus impetu, aliquid secretioris latebrae ad
colligendum animum desideravit; et, offerente Phaonte
liberto suburbanum suum inter Salariam et Nomentanam
viam circa quartum miliarium, ut erat, nudo pede atque tuni-
catus, paenulam obsoleti coloris superinduit; adopertoque   5
capite et ante faciem obtento sudario, equum inscendit,
quattuor solis comitantibus, inter quos et Sporus erat.
statimque tremore terrae et fulgure adverso pavefactus,

audiit ex proximis castris clamorem militum, et sibi adversa
et Galbae prospera ominantium, etiam ex obviis viatoribus 10
quendam dicentem 'hi Neronem persequuntur', alium scis-
citantem 'ecquid in urbe novi de Nerone?' equo autem
odore abiecti in via cadaveris consternato, detecta facie
agnitus est a quodam missicio praetoriano et salutatus.

Suetonius, Nero 48

1 List the information given. Would you call this narrative
   precise? Or is there a confusing or excessive amount of
   detail?
2 What do we gather about (*a*) the character of Nero, and
   (*b*) the attitude of the author towards Nero, from this
   extract? Illustrate your answer from the text.
3 How much could be described as historical fact and how
   much artistic elaboration? What are the key words in the
   non-factual parts, and what might they tell us about
   Suetonius' *intention*?
4 How could you describe Suetonius' prose-style? The
   above extract contains two sentences – do they reveal a
   studied or a rather careless style? Illustrate your answer.

7   *The murder of Cicero*

(A)

M. Cicero pro certo habens, id quod erat, non magis se
Antonio eripi quam Caesari Cassium et Brutum posse,
primo in Tusculanum fugerat, inde transversis itineribus in
Formianum, ut a Caieta navem conscensurus, proficis-
citur. unde aliquoties in altum provectum cum modo 5
venti adversi rettulissent, modo ipse iactationem navis
caeco volvente fluctu pati non posset, taedium tandem eum
et fugae et vitae cepit, regressusque ad superiorem villam,
quae paulo plus mille passibus a mari abest, 'moriar' inquit
'in patria saepe servata.' satis constat servos fortiter fide- 10
literque paratos fuisse ad dimicandum; ipsum deponi
lecticam et quietos pati, quod sors iniqua cogeret, iussisse.
prominenti ex lectica praebentique inmotam cervicem caput
praecisum est. nec satis stolidae crudelitati militum fuit;

manus quoque, scripsisse aliquid in Antonium expro- 15
brantes, praeciderunt. ita relatum caput ad Antonium
iussuque eius inter duas manus in rostris positum, ubi ille
consul, ubi saepe consularis, ubi eo ipso anno adversus
Antonium, quanta nulla umquam humana vox, cum ad-
miratione eloquentiae auditus fuerat.   20

Livy, *Periochae* 120 fr. 60

(B)

M. Cicero C. Popilium Laenatem non minore cura quam
eloquentia defendit eumque salvum ad penates suos
remisit. hic Popilius postea nec re nec verbo a Cicerone
laesus ultro M. Antonium rogavit ut ad illum proscriptum
persequendum et iugulandum mitteretur, impetratisque 5
detestabilis ministerii partibus gaudio exultans Caietam
cucurrit et virum iugulum praebere iussit ac protinus caput
Romanae eloquentiae et pacis clarissimam dexteram per
summum et securum otium amputavit eaque sarcina tamquam opimis spoliis alacer in urbem reversus est: neque 10
enim scelestum portanti onus succurrit illud se caput ferre,
quod pro capite eius quondam peroraverat. invalidae ad hoc
monstrum suggillandum litterae, quoniam qui talem
Ciceronis casum satis digne deplorare possit, alius Cicero
non extat.   15

Valerius Maximus, v. 3, 4 (with omissions)

9. *sarcina, -ae f.*: bundle, load.
10. *spolia opima*: spoils taken from an enemy general when slain by the
commander of a Roman army. A rare and great honour.
13. *suggillo (1)*: insult, abuse.

1 In these two accounts, both authors are basically telling
   the same story, but they approach it in different ways.
   Suggest a title for each piece which takes into account the
   different approach each author has made to his narration
   of the murder.
2 In what respects of *detail* do the two accounts differ?
3 Do both writers have the same *attitude* to their stories?
   If so, what is it? When is it apparent?
4 Against whom, in each case, does the writer aim his
   accusation for the murder of Cicero?

5 Which account would you call more dramatic? Which more emotional? In which is the actual murder more vividly portrayed?

6 Both authors end these pieces with very similar thoughts, but each is angled differently. Which is more forceful, which more clever?

8 Mezentius mourns over his son Lausus

Lausus has been mortally wounded in the act of saving his father Mezentius from the sword of Aeneas. Mezentius, nursing his own wound beside the Tiber, is unaware that his son has died.

> Multa super Lauso rogitat, multumque remittit
> qui revocent maestique ferant mandata parentis.
> at Lausum socii exanimem super arma ferebant
> flentes, ingentem atque ingenti vulnere victum.
> agnovit longe gemitum praesaga mali mens.   5
> canitiem multo deformat pulvere et ambas
> ad caelum tendit palmas et corpore inhaeret.
> 'tantane me tenuit vivendi, nate, voluptas,
> ut pro me hostili paterer succedere dextrae,
> quem genui? tuane haec genitor per vulnera servor   10
> morte tua vivens? heu, nunc misero mihi demum
> exitium infelix, nunc alte vulnus adactum!
> idem ego, nate, tuum maculavi crimine nomen,
> pulsus ob invidiam solio sceptrisque paternis.
> debueram patriae poenas odiisque meorum: 15
> omnis per mortis animam sontem ipse dedissem!
> nunc vivo neque adhuc homines lucemque relinquo.
> sed linquam.'   Virgil, *Aeneid* x. 839–56

1 How would you describe the feeling of this passage?

2 Look up Mezentius in the *Oxford Classical Dictionary* and explain vv. 8–15. How does Mezentius' past history aid comprehension of this passage?

3 What is the effect of the rhythm of v. 4? In what way is the sound expressive? Comment also on the repetition.

4 What effect does the monosyllabic ending have in v. 5?
   Are there any irregularities in v. 11? Discuss the sound of
   the latter half of the verse.
5 What is implied by the pause after *sed linquam* in v. 17?
   Does it form a good ending to Mezentius' speech?

9 *A sound analysis*

For any poet, and especially an oral poet like Homer, the
sound of the verse is an important consideration. There are
many ways in which one can attempt to analyse the sound of a
poem, and one such way is by an examination of the sequences
of *phonemes*, which are significant groups of repeated sounds.
Read this passage aloud several times paying especial attention
to the sound of the words, and then answer the questions. (See
further A. B. Lord in *A Companion to Homer*, pp. 200 ff.)

Ἀλλ' ὅτε δὴ πόρον ἷξον ἐϋρρεῖος ποταμοῖο,
Ξάνθου δινήεντος, ὃν ἀθάνατος τέκετο Ζεύς,
ἔνθα διατμήξας τοὺς μὲν πεδίονδε δίωκε
πρὸς πόλιν, ᾗ περ Ἀχαιοὶ ἀτυζόμενοι φοβέοντο
ἤματι τῷ προτέρῳ, ὅτε μαίνετο φαίδιμος Ἕκτωρ·   5
τῇ ῥ' οἵ γε προχέοντο πεφυζότες, ἠέρα δ' Ἥρη
πίτνα πρόσθε βαθεῖαν ἐρυκέμεν· ἡμίσεες δὲ
ἐς ποταμὸν εἰλεῦντο βαθύρροον ἀργυροδίνην,
ἐν δ' ἔπεσον μεγάλῳ πατάγῳ, βράχε δ' αἰπὰ ῥέεθρα,
ὄχθαι δ' ἀμφὶ περὶ μεγάλ' ἴαχον· οἱ δ' ἀλαλητῷ   10
ἔννεον ἔνθα καὶ ἔνθα, ἑλισσόμενοι περὶ δίνας.
ὡς δ' ὅθ' ὑπὸ ῥιπῆς πυρὸς ἀκρίδες ἠερέθονται
φευγέμεναι ποταμόνδε· τὸ δὲ φλέγει ἀκάματον πῦρ
ὅρμενον ἐξαίφνης, ταὶ δὲ πτώσσουσι καθ' ὕδωρ·
ὡς ὑπ' Ἀχιλλῆος Ξάνθου βαθυδινήεντος   15
πλῆτο ῥόος κελάδων ἐπιμὶξ ἵππων τε καὶ ἀνδρῶν.

                                     Homer, *Iliad* XXI. 1–16

1 The river Xanthos is obviously an important subject in the
   first lines. Look for other ξ and α-ν-τ (θ) sounds; and look
   also for π-(ρ)-ο and τ-α-μ in ποταμός.
2 Follow the repetition of the τ-κ in τέκετο (v. 2) through to
   the climax (with what word?) in v. 5.

9

3 Another important subject is ἠέρα (v. 6). Trace the growth of the use of the sounds in this word from vv. 1–7.

4 From vv. 7–14, trace the development of π-υ-ρ sounds from the key word πυρός in v. 12.

5 What vowel sounds predominate in vv. 9–10, and what is their effect?

6 Look for any other groupings of sounds which seem to you significant.

7 From this small study of phonemes, what conclusions would you draw (*a*) about the extent to which such a study has helped you appreciate this passage, and (*b*) about the helpfulness of an approach such as this?

10 *A Roman heroine*

C. Plinius Nepoti Suo S.

Aegrotabat Caecina Paetus maritus eius, aegrotabat et filius, uterque mortifere, ut videbatur. filius decessit eximia pulchritudine pari verecundia, et parentibus non minus ob alia carus quam quod filius erat. huic illa ita funus paravit, ita duxit exsequias, ut ignoraret maritus; quin 5
immo quotiens cubiculum eius intraret, vivere filium atque etiam commodiorem esse simulabat, ac persaepe interro-ganti, quid ageret puer, respondebat; 'bene quievit, libenter cibum sumpsit.' deinde, cum diu cohibitae lacrimae vin-cerent prorumperentque, egrediebatur: tunc se dolori 10
dabat; satiata siccis oculis composito vultu redibat, tam-quam orbitatem foris reliquisset. praeclarum quidem illud eiusdem, ferrum stringere, perfodere pectus, extrahere pugionem, porrigere marito, addere vocem immortalem ac paene divinam: 'Paete, non dolet.' sed tamen ista facienti, 15
ista dicenti, gloria et aeternitas ante oculos erant; quo maius est sine praemio aeternitatis, sine praemio gloriae, abdere lacrimas operire luctum, amissoque filio matrem adhuc agere.   Pliny, *Epistulae* III. 16 (part)

1 Comment on the narrative style of this letter. Is it simple and direct – or contrived and complex? Or neither?

2   Is the language emotional or restrained? Give examples to
    illustrate your answer.
3   What point does Pliny finish by making? Does this add
    something to the story, or rather dampen its effect?
4   What impression does this passage convey of the character
    of the author?

11   *The beginning of the end*

Ὅτι μὲν ὑμεῖς, ὦ ἄνδρες Ἀθηναῖοι, πεπόνθατε ὑπὸ τῶν
ἐμῶν κατηγόρων, οὐκ οἶδα· ἐγὼ δ' οὖν καὶ αὐτὸς ὑπ' αὐτῶν
ὀλίγου ἐμαυτοῦ ἐπελαθόμην, οὕτω πιθανῶς ἔλεγον. καίτοι
ἀληθές γε ὡς ἔπος εἰπεῖν οὐδὲν εἰρήκασιν. μάλιστα δὲ αὐτῶν
ἓν ἐθαύμασα τῶν πολλῶν ὧν ἐψεύσαντο, τοῦτο ἐν ᾧ ἔλεγον   5
ὡς χρῆν ὑμᾶς εὐλαβεῖσθαι μὴ ὑπ' ἐμοῦ ἐξαπατηθῆτε ὡς
δεινοῦ ὄντος λέγειν. τὸ γὰρ μὴ αἰσχυνθῆναι ὅτι αὐτίκα ὑπ'
ἐμοῦ ἐξελεγχθήσονται ἔργῳ, ἐπειδὰν μηδ' ὁπωστιοῦν
φαίνωμαι δεινὸς λέγειν, τοῦτό μοι ἔδοξεν αὐτῶν ἀναισχυν-
τότατον εἶναι, εἰ μὴ ἄρα δεινὸν καλοῦσιν οὗτοι λέγειν τὸν   10
τἀληθῆ λέγοντα· εἰ μὲν γὰρ τοῦτο λέγουσιν, ὁμολογοίην ἂν
ἔγωγε οὐ κατὰ τούτους εἶναι ῥήτωρ. οὗτοι μὲν οὖν, ὥσπερ
ἐγὼ λέγω, ἤ τι ἢ οὐδὲν ἀληθὲς εἰρήκασιν, ὑμεῖς δέ μου ἀκού-
σεσθε πασαν τὴν ἀλήθειαν — οὐ μέντοι μὰ Δία, ὦ ἄνδρες
Ἀθηναῖοι, κεκαλλιεπημένους γε λόγους, ὥσπερ οἱ τούτων,   15
ῥήμασί τε καὶ ὀνόμασιν οὐδὲ κεκοσμημένους, ἀλλ' ἀκού-
σεσθε εἰκῇ λεγόμενα τοῖς ἐπιτυχοῦσιν ὀνόμασιν — πιστεύω
γὰρ δίκαια εἶναι ἃ λέγω — καὶ μηδεὶς ὑμῶν προσδοκησάτω
ἄλλως· οὐδὲ γὰρ ἂν δήπου πρέποι, ὦ ἄνδρες, τῇδε τῇ
ἡλικίᾳ ὥσπερ μειρακίῳ πλάττοντι λόγους εἰς ὑμᾶς εἰσιέναι.   20
                              Plato, *Apology* 17a–c5

1   Socrates is not popular in certain quarters of Athens, and is
    facing a death penalty. Do you feel the content and tone of
    these, his opening words of defence, to be consonant with
    a desire to get off the charge?
2   What is the tone of the first two sentences, and how does
    the third alter it?
3   In sentences 4–5 (ll. 4–11), what do you think Socrates'
    opponents meant by calling him δεινὸς λέγειν? If Socrates

is not δεινός in that sense, could you suggest one way in which he is?

4 What accusations against himself, real or implied, does Socrates turn round against his accusers in sentence 7 (ll. 12–19)?

5 Bearing in mind Socrates' reputation, say why sentence 8 (ll. 19–20) would have given particular offence to his accusers.

6 Do you think Socrates is being courageous, or foolhardy, or both?

7 Does the subject matter read as if it is off-the-cuff, or well prepared? Can you say the same for the style? What implications does this have for the truth of Plato's reporting?

12 *The news of Lake Trasimene*

Romae ad primum nuntium cladis eius cum ingenti terrore ac tumultu concursus in forum populi est factus. matronae vagae per vias, quae repens clades allata quaeve fortuna exercitus esset, obvios percontantur; et cum frequentis contionis modo turba in comitium et curiam versa magistratus 5 vocaret, tandem haud multo ante solis occasum M. Pomponius praetor 'pugna' inquit 'magna victi sumus'. et quamquam nihil certius ex eo auditum est, tamen alius ab alio impleti rumoribus domos referunt: consulem cum magna parte copiarum caesum; superesse paucos aut fuga passim 10 per Etruriam sparsos aut captos ab hoste. quot casus exercitus victi fuerant, tot in curas distracti animi eorum erant quorum propinqui sub C. Flaminio consule meruerant, ignorantium quae cuiusque suorum fortuna esset; nec quisquam satis certum habet quid aut speret aut timeat. postero 15 ac deinceps aliquot diebus ad portas maior prope mulierum quam virorum multitudo stetit, aut suorum aliquem aut nuntios de iis opperiens; circumfundebanturque obviis sciscitantes neque avelli, utique ab notis, priusquam ordine omnia inquisissent, poterant. inde varios voltus digre- 20 dientium ab nuntiis cerneres, ut cuique laeta aut tristia nuntiabantur, gratulantesque aut consolantes redeuntibus domos circumfusos. feminarum praecipue et gaudia insignia

erant et luctus. unam in ipsa porta sospiti filio repente
oblatam in complexu eius exspirasse ferunt; alteram, cui 25
mors filii falso nuntiata erat, maestam sedentem domi, ad
primum conspectum redeuntis filii gaudio nimio exani-
matam.   Livy XXII. 7. 6–13

1   How effectively and quickly does Livy set the scene, the
    place, occasion and circumstances? Would 'dramatic' be a
    suitable description of the Latin in the first four sentences?
    What is the effect of the brief announcement of M.
    Pomponius?
2   How well, and by what method, is the panic and confusion
    of the people depicted? Does the narrative move quickly?
3   How far does Livy succeed in putting the reader on the
    spot as events happened? What particular touches help to
    make the picture come to life?
4   Examine Livy's variation of tenses. What is his purpose in
    this variation?
5   What is the difference between factual reporting and
    history? How much of what Livy writes is the reporting
    of facts, and how much his own comment? What does the
    nature of the material that does not advance the narrative
    suggest about the author's interest in history?
6   Quintilian claims that Livy depicted emotions ('especially
    the "softer" emotions') as no other historian. What signs
    of the master-touch would you select for comment from this
    passage?

13   The hand of fate

Adrastus, purified by Croesus from a previous murder, has
accidently killed Croesus' son. Croesus had put him into
Adrastus' care during a hunt, as he had had a dream that his
son would be killed by spear-point.

Παρῆσαν δὲ μετὰ τοῦτο οἱ Λυδοὶ φέροντες τὸν νεκρόν,
ὄπισθε δὲ εἵπετό οἱ ὁ φονεύς. στὰς δὲ οὗτος πρὸ τοῦ νεκροῦ
παρεδίδου ἑωυτὸν Κροίσῳ προτείνων τὰς χεῖρας, ἐπικατα-
σφάξαι μιν κελεύων τῷ νεκρῷ, λέγων τήν τε προτέρην
ἑωυτοῦ συμφορήν, καὶ ὡς ἐπ᾽ ἐκείνῃ τὸν καθήραντα ἀπολω-   5

λεκὼς εἴη, οὐδέ οἱ εἴη βιώσιμον. Κροῖσος δὲ τούτων ἀκούσας
τόν τε Ἄδρηστον κατοικτίρει, καίπερ ἐὼν ἐν κακῷ οἰκηίῳ
τοσούτῳ, καὶ λέγει πρὸς αὐτόν· 'ἔχω, ὦ ξεῖνε, παρὰ σεῦ
πᾶσαν τὴν δίκην, ἐπειδὴ σεωυτοῦ καταδικάζεις θάνατον.
εἶς δὲ οὐ σύ μοι τοῦδε τοῦ κακοῦ αἴτιος, εἰ μὴ ὅσον ἀέκων   10
ἐξεργάσαο, ἀλλὰ θεῶν κού τις, ὅς μοι καὶ πάλαι προεσήμαινε
τὰ μέλλοντα ἔσεσθαι.' Κροῖσος μέν νυν ἔθαψε, ὡς οἶκος ἦν,
τὸν ἑωυτοῦ παῖδα· Ἄδρηστος δὲ ὁ Γορδίεω τοῦ Μίδεω,
οὗτος δὴ ὁ φονεὺς μὲν τοῦ ἑωυτοῦ ἀδελφεοῦ γενόμενος,
φονεὺς δὲ τοῦ καθήραντος, ἐπείτε ἡσυχίη τῶν ἀνθρώπων   15
ἐγένετο περὶ τὸ σῆμα, συγγινωσκόμενος ἀνθρώπων εἶναι
τῶν αὐτὸς ᾔδεε βαρυσυμφορώτατος, ἐπικατασφάζει τῷ
τύμβῳ ἑωυτόν.   Herodotus I. 45

1 What is the key word in the first sentence? Where does it
   come, and why?
2 Analyse sentence 2 (ll. 2–6). Why is the main verb im-
   perfect? Look for triplet constructions – do they build up
   to a satisfying climax?
3 What would be lost to the passage if Croesus' words of
   reply were omitted?
4 In sentence 7 (ll. 13–18), give examples of irony and
   anaphora. From συγγινωσκόμενος to the end, what feeling
   do the long words impart? Why does Herodotus use the
   word order he does from συγγινωσκόμενος to βαρυσυμφορώτατος?
5 Do you think that this passage illustrates convincingly
   why Herodotus was called Ὁμηρικώτατος?

14 *The lover campaigns*

Militat omnis amans, et habet sua castra Cupido;
   Attice, crede mihi, militat omnis amans.
quae bello est habilis, Veneri quoque convenit aetas:
   turpe senex miles, turpe senilis amor.
quos petiere duces annos in milite forti,   5
   hos petit in socio bella puella viro:
pervigilant ambo, terra requiescit uterque;
   ille fores dominae servat, at ille ducis.

militis officium longa est via: mitte puellam,
  strenuus exempto fine sequetur amans;   10
ibit in adversos montes duplicataque nimbo
  flumina, congestas exteret ille nives,
nec freta pressurus tumidos causabitur Euros
  aptaque verrendis sidera quaeret aquis.
quis nisi vel miles vel amans et frigora noctis   15
  et denso mixtas perferet imbre nives?
mittitur infestos alter speculator in hostes,
  in rivale oculos alter, ut hoste, tenet.
ille graves urbes, hic durae limen amicae
  obsidet; hic portas frangit, at ille fores.   20

                                   Ovid, *Amores* I. 9. 1–20

1 Analyse the structure of the whole passage. Does the
   comparison appear carefully planned or spontaneous?
2 Discuss the purpose of the repetition in vv. 1 and 2.
3 Is there any difference between *portas* and *fores* in v. 20?
4 Is the lover/soldier image successfully developed? Where
   are the two ideas brought together for the first time? In
   what couplet is the contrast expressed the greatest number
   of times?
5 Is Ovid open to the charge of monotony here?
6 On the basis of these conclusions, does the poetry as a
   whole, and the language in particular, strike you as
   passionate and emotional, or rather sophisticated, witty
   and ingenious? Illustrate your answer.

15 *Agricola's last hours*

After a distinguished military career in the latter part of which
he incurred the jealousy of the emperor Domitian, Agricola
dies.

Finis vitae eius nobis luctuosus, amicis tristis, extraneis
etiam ignotisque non sine cura fuit. vulgus quoque et hic
aliud agens populus et ventitavere ad domum et per fora et
circulos locuti sunt; nec quisquam audita morte Agricolae
aut laetatus est aut statim oblitus. augebat miserationem   5

constans rumor veneno interceptum: nobis nihil comperti adfirmare ausim. ceterum per omnem valetudinem eius crebrius quam ex more principatus per nuntios visentis et libertorum primi et medicorum intimi venere, sive cura illud sive inquisitio erat. supremo quidem die momenta 10 ipsa deficientis per dispositos cursores nuntiata constabat, nullo credente sic adcelerari quae tristis audiret. speciem tamen doloris animi vultu prae se tulit, securus iam odii et qui facilius dissimularet gaudium quam metum. satis constabat lecto testamento Agricolae, quo coheredem optimae 15 uxori et piissimae filiae Domitianum scripsit, laetatum eum velut honore iudicioque. tam caeca et corrupta mens adsiduis adulationibus erat, ut nesciret a bono patre non scribi heredem nisi malum principem.   Tacitus, *Agricola* XLIII

12–13. *speciem...tulit*: sc. Domitian, who was jealous of Agricola.
17. *velut honore iudicioque*: 'as if it were a compliment and a free choice'.

1   What does the author intend us to feel about (*a*) the death of Agricola and (*b*) the actions of the emperor Domitian?
2   Describe Tacitus' *style* in this chapter. Does the language rise to the occasion (this is an important climax in the biography of Agricola), or is the author being deliberately restrained and matter-of-fact?
3   What is given more weight in this chapter – the death of Agricola or the way it affects the emperor? What is the author most anxious to say?
4   How much evidence can you see of careful composition? Did Tacitus spend a long time on this section, or is it quite ordinary prose?

16   *The power of love*

Quicumque ille fuit, puerum qui pinxit Amorem,
    nonne putas miras hunc habuisse manus?
is primum vidit sine sensu vivere amantis,
    et levibus curis magna perire bona.
idem non frustra ventosas addidit alas,   5
    fecit et humano corde volare deum:

scilicet alterna quoniam iactamur in unda,
  nostraque non ullis permanet aura locis.
et merito hamatis manus est armata sagittis,
  et pharetra ex umero Cnosia utroque iacet: 10
ante ferit quoniam tuti quam cernimus hostem,
  nec quisquam ex illo vulnere sanus abit.
in me tela manent, manet et puerilis imago:
  sed certe pennas perdidit ille suas;
evolat heu nostro quoniam de pectore nusquam,   15
  assiduusque meo sanguine bella gerit.
quid tibi iucundum est siccis habitare medullis?
  si pudor est, alio traice tela tua!
intactos isto satius temptare veneno:
  non ego, sed tenuis vapulat umbra mea.   20
quam si perdideris, quis erit qui talia cantet,
  (haec mea Musa levis gloria magna tua est),
qui caput et digitos et lumina nigra puellae
  et canat ut soleant molliter ire pedes?

Propertius II. 12

5. *ventosas*: 'swift as the wind'.
8. *nostra aura*: i.e. the breeze before which we sail.
10. *Cnosia*: Cretan; Cretan archers were famous for their skill.
11. *tuti*: because 'forewarned is forearmed'.
20. *umbra mea*: i.e. 'only a shadow of me' (I am as good as dead).

1 What is the poem about? Is the title given above appropriate? 'It is only formally a love poem' (Quinn). If you agree, say what else it could be.
2 Divide the poem up into blocks of sense. What are the main steps in the poet's argument? Would you call the poem tightly constructed?
3 What, in the light of what follows, is the importance of *Amor* and *puer* in the first line? How is the idea carried through?
4 What is the meaning of v. 5, and how is the imagery picked up again?
5 What do you notice about the *form* or structure of vv. 5–12 which is worthy of comment?
6 Is the feeling uniform throughout, or rather flippant in one place and serious in another?
7 What is the purpose of the last four lines? Do they form an effective and suitable ending?

Compare the following translations:

Love as a boy – what artist painted this?
A master's hand (must we not think?) was his.
He saw how lovers live with senses blurred,
Great joys being lost and trivial cares incurred.
Then wind-blown wings he added, as was right,   5
And showed the fickle-hearted god in flight:
For tossed, you know, on see-saw waves we ride,
And nowhere does our shifting breeze abide.
As weapons in his hand barbed shafts are best;
The Cretan quiver on his back must rest;   10
Since, ere we think, he strikes, a hidden foe,
And none escapes unwounded from the blow.
But in my case, though still the semblance clings
Of boy and bowman, he has lost his wings:
For lodged, alas, within my heart he plies   15
His warfare in my blood, and never flies.
Is this your chosen home, a bloodless heart?
Elsewhere, in honour, take and aim your dart.
Fresh victims for your venom you should boast:
In me you flog an unsubstantial ghost.   20
Slight is my muse, yet no small fame to you:
If you destroy me, who will sing so true
My girl's black eyes, her fingers, and her head,
And how her feet most delicately tread?

A. E. Watts (Penguin Books 1966)

(B)

I

Whoever first love as a child portrayed,
think you not he had a cunning hand?
He first saw how lovers senseless live,
by trivial dealing profitless distraught.   4

Pertinent, too, the windy wings he added then,
devising a god that flits within man's heart.
(Plainly conflicting ways the eddy tosses us;
ours is a breeze whose set does not abide.)   8

18

Likewise just the barbed tip that arms his hand,
the Cretan quiver from each shoulder hanging.
(Against foe that unseen strikes no staying safe;
none whom he hits makes off unmaimed.)   12

II

In me the boyish guise, the pointed arrow holds,
but those wings of his love's lost somehow:
from my heart he never flies away; in my
veins I feel love's unrelenting war.   16

III

Why dwell in dried-out bones? What pleasure there?
Have you no shame? Aim your shaft another place –
against the unafflicted the poison better turned;
not me but my wasted shadow they assail.   20

That destroyed, who will be your singer then?
(My frivolous Muse has brought you much renown.)
And who'll my black-eyed mistress sing, head and toe,
when she walks, how her steps do melting go?   24
                    K. Quinn, *Latin Explorations* 169

1 Why does Quinn divide his translation into three sections,
   and six stanzas? Do they correspond to the sense-blocks
   you have listed?
2 Judging from your analysis of the poem, which translation
   has caught the feeling of the original better?
3 What is the major difference between the two translations?
4 Do rhyming couplets help such translation to succeed, or
   rather stand in the way of its success? Would you opt for
   blank verse or non-rhyming quatrains in order to achieve
   more freedom of expression?
5 Which translation, *qua* translation, is better, and which is
   better *poetry*?

17 *Sound and sense*

The elegiac metre seems to have been very suitable for epigrams. Here are a number, all of quite different levels of intent. When you have answered the questions, say why this metre was used for this purpose. Learn by heart the epigram which appeals to you most.

(A)

Ὑψίκομον παρὰ τάνδε καθίζεο φωνήεσσαν
  φρίσσουσαν πυκινοῖς κῶνον ὑπὸ Ζεφύροις,
καί σοι καχλάζουσιν ἐμοῖς παρὰ νάμασι σύριγξ
  θελγομένων ἄξει κῶμα κατὰ βλεφάρων.

Plato, *Oxford Book of Greek Verse* 450

1 The main phonemes (see glossary of technical terms, p. 130, and cf. no. 9) in vv. 1–2 are the π-ς group, involving π, φ, ψ, ς, ʒ, and to a lesser extent ω, κ. Examine the distribution of these and trace the changes which occur in vv. 3–4.

2 How effective do you find the conjunction of sound with sense in this poem? Illustrate your answer from the text.

3 What predominant feeling is conveyed to the reader?

(B)

Σῶμα μὲν ἀλλοδαπὴ κεύθει κόνις, ἐν δέ σε πόντῳ,
  Κλείσθενες, Εὐξείνῳ μοῖρ' ἔκιχεν θανάτου
πλαζόμενον· γλυκεροῦ δὲ μελίφρονος οἴκαδε νόστου
  ἤμπλακες, οὐδ' ἵκευ Χῖον ἐς ἀμφιρύτην.

Simonides, *Diehl* 135

4. ἵκευ: 'you reached'.

1 Follow and discuss the changing pattern of phonemes.

2 How does the use of long words echo and help the sense?

3 Do you find the sentiment effusive, or restrained? Does this help or hinder the force of the poem?

20

(c)

Οὐκ εἴμ’ οὐδ’ ἐτέων δύο κεἴκοσι, καὶ κοπιῶ ζῶν.
 Ὤρωτες, τί κακὸν τοῦτο; τί με φλέγετε;
ἢν γὰρ ἐγώ τι πάθω, τί ποιήσετε; δῆλον, Ἔρωτες,
 ὡς τὸ πάρος παίξεσθ’ ἄφρονες ἀστραγάλοις.

Asclepiades, *Oxford Book of Greek Verse* 529

1 What is the tone of this poem? How does it differ from the
 above two?
2 Can you find any significant groupings of phonemes?
3 Is this writer genuinely concerned about his fortune?

(D)

Πῖνε καὶ εὐφραίνου· τί γὰρ αὔριον, ἢ τί τὸ μέλλον,
 οὐδεὶς γινώσκει. μὴ τρέχε, μὴ κοπία,
ὡς δύνασαι, χάρισαι, μετάδος, φάγε, θνητὰ λογίζου·
 τὸ ζῆν τοῦ μὴ ζῆν οὐδὲν ὅλως ἀπέχει.
πᾶς ὁ βίος τοιόσδε, ῥοπὴ μόνον· ἂν προλάβῃς, σού,   5
 ἂν δὲ θάνῃς, ἑτέρου πάντα, σὺ δ’ οὐδὲν ἔχεις.

Anonymous, *Oxford Book of Greek Verse* 695

1 To which of the other poems is the style of this one more
 akin?
2 Is the tone flippant, or serious – or what?
3 Does the style suit the subject and its handling?

18 *How many kisses...?*

Quaeris, quot mihi basiationes
tuae, Lesbia, sint satis superque.
quam magnus numerus Libyssae harenae
lasarpiciferis iacet Cyrenis
oraclum Iovis inter aestuosi   5

et Batti veteris sacrum sepulcrum;
aut quam sidera multa, cum tacet nox,
furtivos hominum vident amores:
tam te basia multa basiare
vesano satis et super Catullo est,   10
quae nec pernumerare curiosi
possint nec mala fascinare lingua.

Catullus VII

4. *lasarpiciferis*: bearing the *laserpicium*, a plant (used for medicinal purposes) growing in Cyrenaica. A staple export of Cyrene.
6. *Batti*: Battus was the legendary founder and first king of Cyrene.

1 What is the sense of the poem? On first impressions, is the poem at all serious? Or is it a *jeu d'esprit*, a mere literary exercise?
2 Does closer analysis reveal any subtleties? With the help of a dictionary, discuss the effect on the atmosphere of the poem of words such as *Libyssae*, *lasarpiciferis*, *Batti*, *Cyrenis*. In Latin poetry we often meet lists of place-names – what purpose, if any, does the list serve here?
3 Catullus is called *doctus* by Martial. What could this mean?
4 Is your final impression that the poem is successful? Do we receive the impression that Catullus really loves his Lesbia? Do his extravagant comparisons convince? Or does the whole thing give the impression that the poet is being 'clever' in an 'occasional' poem?

19 *Marcellus*

Cicero praises the clemency of Marcellus, the general who captured Syracuse in 212 B.C.

Denique ille ipse M. Marcellus, cuius in Sicilia virtutem hostes, misericordiam victi, fidem ceteri Siculi perspexerunt, non solum sociis in eo bello consuluit, verum etiam superatis hostibus temperavit. urbem pulcherrimam Syracusas, – quae cum manu munitissima esset, tum loci natura terra ac   5
mari clauderetur, – cum vi consilioque cepisset, non solum incolumem passus est esse, sed ita reliquit ornatam ut esset idem monumentum victoriae, mansuetudinis, continentiae, cum homines viderent et quid expugnasset et quibus peper-

cisset et quae reliquisset: tantum ille honorem habendum 10
Siciliae putavit ut ne hostium quidem urbem ex sociorum
insula tollendam arbitraretur. itaque ad omnis res sic illa
provincia semper usi sumus ut, quicquid ex sese posset
efferre, id non apud nos nasci, sed domi nostrae conditum
iam putaremus. quando illa frumentum quod deberet non 15
ad diem dedit? quando id quod opus esse putaret non ultro
pollicita est? quando id quod imperaretur recusavit? itaque
ille M. Cato Sapiens cellam penariam rei publicae nostrae,
nutricem plebis Romanae Siciliam nominabat.

Cicero, *In Verrem* II. 2. 4–5 (70 B.C.)

1 Summarise in a few sentences what Cicero is saying.
2 Examine the first sentence. Read it aloud several times.
  What effect does the word order produce?
3 What is the purpose of the parenthesis in sentence 2
  (ll. 5–6)? Why is the second sentence so long, and the
  last five so much shorter?
4 Study the structure of sentences 2 and 3 (ll. 4–12; 12–15);
  is there any striking balance here?
5 What is the orator's method of showing Marcellus'
  clemency?
6 Is there any redundancy of expression here? If so, is it bad
  writing, or does it serve a purpose?
7 All in all, is this an effective piece of oratory? Is the
  emotional temperature high or low? Is it even throughout,
  or does it fluctuate?

20 *Horrida tempestas*

Horrida tempestas caelum contraxit et imbres
    nivesque deducunt Iovem; nunc mare, nunc silvae
Threicio Aquilone sonant: rapiamus, amici,
    occasionem de die, dumque virent genua
et decet, obducta solvatur fronte senectus.   5
    tu vina Torquato move consule pressa meo:
cetera mitte loqui: deus haec fortasse benigna
    reducet in sedem vice. nunc et Achaemenio
perfundi nardo iuvat et fide Cyllenea

levare diris pectora sollicitudinibus;   10
nobilis ut grandi cecinit Centaurus alumno:
  'invicte, mortalis dea nate puer Thetide,
te manet Assaraci tellus, quam frigida parvi
  findunt Scamandri flumina lubricus et Simois;
unde tibi reditum certo subtemine Parcae   15
  rupere, nec mater domum caerula te revehet.
illic omne malum vino cantuque levato,
  deformis aegrimoniae dulcibus alloquiis.'

Horace, *Epode* XIII

11. *nobilis . . . Centaurus*: i.e. Chiron, tutor of Achilles.

1 In what mood is this poem written? Is it light-hearted,
witty, jolly – or rather reflective and serious, or neither?
2 How many blocks of sense go into the composition of
this poem? Are they harmoniously united, or is the balance
unsatisfactory?
3 How does *sound* help in the description of the storm?
4 What are the key words in what the poet is saying, and how
are they illustrated/reinforced by the 'myth' (vv. 11ff.)?
5 Why is *Achilles* (*dea nate . . . Thetide*, v. 12) chosen as an
illustration of Horace's philosophy in this poem? Is the
myth merely an encouragement to 'never mind the
weather', or does it say something deeper? To what might
the storm refer, other than literally to bad weather? In the
light of this, does *rapiamus, amici,* / *occasionem de die*
(vv. 3–4) refer to one rainy day in particular – or is it a
general reference?

21 *The cause of man's unhappiness*

Si possent homines, proinde ac sentire videntur
pondus inesse animo quod se gravitate fatiget,
e quibus id fiat causis quoque noscere et unde
tanta mali tamquam moles in pectore constet,
haud ita vitam agerent, ut nunc plerumque videmus   5
quid sibi quisque velit nescire et quaerere semper
commutare locum quasi onus deponere possit.
exit saepe foras magnis ex aedibus ille,

esse domi quem pertaesumst, subitoque revertit,
quippe foris nilo melius qui sentiat esse.   10
currit agens mannos ad villam praecipitanter,
auxilium tectis quasi ferre ardentibus instans;
oscitat extemplo, tetigit cum limina villae,
aut abit in somnum gravis atque oblivia quaerit,
aut etiam properans urbem petit atque revisit.   15
hoc se quisque modo fugit, at quem scilicet, ut fit,
effugere haud potis est, ingratis haeret et odit
propterea, morbi quia causam non tenet aeger;
quam bene si videat, iam rebus quisque relictis
naturam primum studeat cognoscere rerum,   20
temporis aeterni quoniam, non unius horae,
ambigitur status, in quo sit mortalibus omnis
aetas, post mortem quae restat cumque, manenda.

> Lucretius, *De Rerum Natura* III. 1053–75

10. *nilo melius*: 'no better off'.
13. *oscitat*: 'he yawns'.
22. *ambigitur*: tr. 'is at stake'.

1 Summarise the sense; what is the poet's argument?
2 Do you consider the tone bitter, or is Lucretius smiling
   quietly to himself – or neither?
3 List the examples of the malaise described; are they well
   chosen and well expressed? What methods of escape are
   employed by the rich man?
4 Look up *mannos* (v. 11) in a dictionary. Has this un-
   common word any special nuance here? Explain *gravis* in
   v. 14. What is its force? What kind of metaphor is
   Lucretius using in v. 22: *status...ambigitur*?
5 Lucretius does not tell us exactly what the cause of all this
   restlessness is – but what do you think he is hinting at?
   What cure does he suggest? Is such a cure impractical?
6 Are sound and rhythm important in this passage?

Compare with vv. 8ff.:

> On that hard Pagan world disgust
> And secret loathing fell.
> Deep weariness and sated lust
> Made human life a hell.   4

In his cool hall, with haggard eyes,
The Roman noble lay;
He drove abroad, in furious guise,
Along the Appian way.   8

He made a feast, drank fierce and fast,
And crowned his hair with flowers –
No easier nor no quicker passed
The impracticable hours.   12

M. Arnold, *Obermann Once More* 93–104

Do you think Arnold had Lucretius in mind when composing these verses?
Do these lines convey a feeling of purposelessness and *ennui*
as successfully as Lucretius' verses?

22   *Gather ye rosebuds...*

Τίς δὲ βίος, τί δε τερπνὸν ἄτερ χρυσῆς Ἀφροδίτης;
    τεθναίην, ὅτε μοι μηκέτι ταῦτα μέλοι,
κρυπταδίη φιλότης καὶ μείλιχα δῶρα καὶ εὐνή·
    οἷ’ ἥβης ἄνθεα γίγνεται ἁρπαλέα
ἀνδράσιν ἠδὲ γυναιξίν· ἐπεὶ δ’ ὀδυνηρὸν ἐπέλθῃ   5
    γῆρας, ὅ τ’ αἰσχρὸν ὁμῶς καὶ κακὸν ἄνδρα τιθεῖ,
αἰεί μιν φρένας ἀμφὶ κακαὶ τείρουσι μέριμναι,
    οὐδ’ αὐγὰς προσορῶν τέρπεται ἠελίου,
ἀλλ’ ἐχθρὸς μὲν παισίν, ἀτίμαστος δὲ γυναιξίν·
    οὕτως ἀργαλέον γῆρας ἔθηκε θεός.   10

Mimnermus, *Oxford Book of Greek Verse* 118

1 Summarise Mimnermus' train of thought. How does the
   last line square with the first?
2 List the 'pleasures' of Aphrodite, and discuss the change of
   vowel sounds in v. 3. Does ἁρπαλέα (v. 4) destroy the tone?
3 List the horrors of old age – what is Mimnermus' attitude
   to it? Comment on the effectiveness of the words he uses
   to describe it.
4 Can you see any reason for the different length of sentence
   throughout the poem?

5 Would you say this was a romantic or sentimental poem, or something quite different?
6 Do you think this poem is complete as it stands?

23   *The rape of Lucretia*

(A)

The story as related by the historian Livy: Sextus Tarquinius, fired with love for Lucretia, wife of Collatinus, is obsessed with the challenge of her chastity. He finally plots the rape and rides into Collatia.

Paucis interiectis diebus Sex. Tarquinius inscio Collatino cum comite uno Collatiam venit. ubi exceptus benigne ab ignaris consilii cum post cenam in hospitale cubiculum deductus esset, amore ardens, postquam satis tuta circa sopitique omnes videbantur, stricto gladio ad dormientem 5 Lucretiam venit sinistraque manu mulieris pectore oppresso 'tace, Lucretia' inquit; 'Sex. Tarquinius sum; ferrum in manu est; moriere, si emiseris vocem.' cum pavida ex somno mulier nullam opem, prope mortem imminentem videret, tum Tarquinius fateri amorem, orare, miscere precibus 10 minas, versare in omnes partes muliebrem animum. ubi obstinatam videbat et ne mortis quidem metu inclinari, addit ad metum dedecus: cum mortua iugulatum servum nudum positurum ait, ut in sordido adulterio necata dicatur. quo terrore cum vicisset obstinatam pudicitiam velut vi victrix 15 libido, profectusque inde Tarquinius ferox expugnato decore muliebri esset, Lucretia maesta tanto malo nuntium Romam eundem ad patrem Ardeamque ad virum mittit, ut cum singulis fidelibus amicis veniant; ita facto maturatoque opus esse; rem atrocem incidisse. 20

Livy I. 58. 1–6

1 Comment on Livy's use of tenses.
2 How effective do you find Tarquinius' words to Lucretia (*tace...vocem*)? Why?
3 Examine the word order in sentence 3 (ll. 8–11). How does each word further the action – or the reader's picture of the action?

4 Discuss the narrative technique of Livy in this passage. His periods are all fairly involved, yet the action moves quickly. How does he achieve this?

(B)

Now Ovid's version:

Hostis ut hospes init penetralia Collatini,
  comiter excipitur: sanguine iunctus erat.
quantum animis erroris inest! parat inscia rerum
  infelix epulas hostibus illa suis.
functus erat dapibus, poscunt sua tempora somnum;   5
  nox erat et tota lumina nulla domo:
surgit et aurata vagina deripit ensem
  et venit in thalamos, nupta pudica, tuos,
utque torum pressit, 'ferrum, Lucretia, mecum est!'
  natus ait regis 'Tarquiniusque loquor.'   10
illa nihil, neque enim vocem viresque loquendi
  aut aliquid toto pectore mentis habet,
sed tremit, ut quondam stabulis deprensa relictis
  parva sub infesto cum iacet agna lupo.
quid faciat? pugnet? vincetur femina pugnans.   15
  clamet? at in dextra, qui vetet, ensis erat.
effugiat? positis urgentur pectora palmis,
  tunc primum externa pectora tacta manu.
instat amans hostis precibus pretioque minisque,
  nec prece nec pretio nec movet ille minis.   20
'nil agis! eripiam' dixit 'per crimina vitam,
  falsus adulterii testis adulter ero:
interimam famulum, cum quo deprensa fereris.'
  succubuit famae victa puella metu.

Ovid, *Fasti* II. 787–810

1 How would you describe the narrative of Ovid in this passage? Is it swift-moving and smoothly flowing, or staccato, perpetually stopping and starting? How would you criticise it?

2 What is the most effective and compelling part of the description of the plight of Lucretia?

3 Does the simile in vv. 13–14 illuminate the picture of the trembling Lucretia – or does it rather interrupt the flow of the narrative? Is it apt?

4 What differences of emphasis are there in these two accounts? Can you suggest reasons for them? What things in particular does Ovid include which are absent from Livy's account?

5 Is there much evidence that Ovid had Livy's account in mind when composing these verses? What similarities of diction are there? Make a list. Does Ovid ever actually seem to versify the prose of Livy?

6 Which account is more *dramatic*? Give reasons for your answer.

7 What thoughts, set off by the account of Livy, occurred to Ovid as good starting points for elaboration? What kind of elaborations does he tend to make?

8 Discuss each of the following points in turn:
(a) 'No prose could equal the swift economy of Ovid.
(b) How well he uses the figures of speech which were the rhetorician's stock-in-trade!
(c) In a scene so dramatic as this neither they nor even the occasional conceits seem forced.' (L. P. Wilkinson, *Ovid Recalled* 284.)

In the light of your observations, criticise the following translation; does this type of verse (a) suit the subject matter, (b) reproduce the flavour of Ovid's elegiacs?

As friend this foe to Collatinus' hall
Was welcomed: kinship made it natural.
Ah, human blindness! All unwitting she
Prepared a banquet for her enemy.
The feast was done, and sleep its hour claimed.   5
Night fell, and through the house no taper flamed.
He rose, and drew his gilded sword, and hied
Straight to the chamber of that innocent bride,
And kneeling on the bed, 'Lucretia', breathed,
''Tis I, Prince Tarquin, with my sword unsheathed!'   10
She nothing spake: she had no power to speak,
Nor any thought in all her heart to seek,

But trembled, as a lamb from sheepfold strayed,
Caught by a wolf, lies under him dismayed.
What could she do? Struggle? She could not win.   15
Cry out? His naked sword would intervene.
Escape? She felt his hands upon her breast,
Never before by hand unlawful pressed.
With prayers and bribes and threats he thought to
    assail,
No prayer or bribe or threat could aught avail.   20
'What use? I'll mingle death and calumny,
Rape, and accuse you of adultery;
A slave I'll kill, say you were caught in sin.'
Fear for her name prevailed, and she gave in.

L. P. Wilkinson, 1955

PART TWO

24 *Heraclitus*

Εἶπέ τις Ἡράκλειτε τεὸν μόρον, ἐς δέ με δάκρυ
ἤγαγεν, ἐμνήσθην δ' ὁσσάκις ἀμφότεροι
ἥλιον ἐν λέσχῃ κατεδύσαμεν· ἀλλὰ σὺ μέν που
ξεῖν' Ἁλικαρνησεῦ τετράπαλαι σποδιή·
αἱ δὲ τεαὶ ζώουσιν ἀηδόνες, ᾗσιν ὁ πάντων   5
ἀρπακτὴς Ἀίδης οὐκ ἐπὶ χεῖρα βαλεῖ.

        Callimachus, *Oxford Book of Greek Verse*, 513

1 What are the subjects of each clause? Can you see a
   logical train of thought?
2 Does Callimachus dwell on any aspect of Heraclitus' death
   for any length of time? How does this affect the tone of
   the poem?
3 ἥλιον ἐν λέσχῃ κατεδύσαμεν (v. 3) has been widely admired.
   Can you suggest why?
4 Use your imagination to say what you think ἀηδόνες (v. 5)
   might stand for. What word breaks the tone of the poem in
   the last line? What image is raised by ἐπὶ χεῖρα βαλεῖ?
5 Does the poem seem to you to be extravagant or sentimental in any way? Do you find it a moving poem, and
   can you say why?
6 Learn the poem by heart.
7 Discuss the merits of the following translation:

They told me, Heraclitus, they told me you were dead;
They brought me bitter news to hear and bitter tears
    to shed.
I wept, as I remembered, how often you and I
Had tired the sun with talking and sent him down the sky.
And now that thou art lying, my dear old Carian guest, 5
A handful of grey ashes, long long ago at rest,
Still are thy pleasant voices, thy nightingales, awake,
For Death, he taketh all away, but them he cannot take.

                William Johnson Cory

25 Two letters

M. Tullius M.f. Cicero s.d. Cn. Pompeio Cn.f. Magno Imperatori.

Ad me autem litteras quas misisti, quamquam exiguam significationem tuae erga me voluntatis habebant, tamen mihi scito iucundas fuisse; nulla enim re tam laetari soleo quam meorum officiorum conscientia; quibus si quando non mutue respondetur, apud me plus officii residere facillime 5
patior. illud non dubito, quin, si te mea summa erga te studia parum mihi adiunxerint, res publica nos inter nos conciliatura coniuncturaque sit. ac ne ignores, quid ego in tuis litteris desiderarim, scribam aperte, sicut et mea natura et nostra amicitia postulat. res eas gessi, quarum aliquam 10
in tuis litteris et nostrae necessitudinis et rei p. causa gratulationem exspectavi; quam ego abs te praetermissam esse arbitror, quod vererere, ne cuius animum offenderes. sed scito ea, quae nos pro salute patriae gessimus, orbis terrae iudicio ac testimonio comprobari. 15

Cicero, *Ad Familiares* v. 7. 2–3

10. *res eas*: referring to the consulship of Cicero in 63 B.C., before this letter was written.

1 Summarise briefly what Cicero is saying.
2 Describe the feeling of the letter – is it intimate, uneasy, tense? Is the tone smug, self-satisfied, offended, frankly vain, cold, bitter – or what?
3 In what spirit did Cicero write the last sentence? What is its effect?
4 Letters are often interesting because they throw light on the writer's character, or his relations with other men. Does this letter have any such interest?
5 Compare this letter with one written to Paetus in 46 B.C. (*Ad Fam.* IX. 20). Are its style and feeling similar? Are you soon aware that you are reading a letter – a friendly, informal exchange – rather than a treatise or a speech?

Dupliciter delectatus sum tuis litteris, et quod ipse risi et quod te intellexi iam posse ridere; me autem a te ut scurram velitem malis oneratum esse non moleste tuli; illud doleo, in ista loca venire me, ut constitueram, non potuisse; habuisses enim non hospitem, sed contubernalem. at quem 5 virum! non eum, quem tu es solitus promulside conficere; integram famem ad ovum adfero, itaque usque ad assum vitulinum opera perducitur. illa mea, quae solebas antea laudare, 'o hominem facilem! o hospitem non gravem!' abierunt; nam omnem nostram de re p. curam, cogitatio- 10 nem de dicenda in senatu sententia, commentationem causarum abiecimus, in Epicuri nos, adversarii nostri, castra coniecimus, nec tamen ad hanc insolentiam, sed ad illam tuam lautitiam, veterem dico, cum in sumptum habebas; etsi numquam plura praedia habuisti. 15

Ad Familiares IX. 20. I

2–3. *ut scurram velitem*: tr. 'as the clown of the troop'. The *scurra* was a sort of professional jester which the Romans had at their dinners.

3. *malis*: apples would have been a likely missile with which to pelt the *scurra*.

6. *promulside*: *hors-d'œuvres*, appetiser before the *cena* began.

7. *ovum*: with which the meal proper opened.

7–8. *assum vitulinum*: roast veal, with which the *cena* ended.

13. *insolentiam*: 'luxury'.

14. *habebas*: sc. *pecuniam*.

15. *plura praedia*: Paetus had been obliged to accept payment of debts in real estate, and so was rich in land, but poor in cash.

26   *Ode to Valgius*

Non semper imbres nubibus hispidos
manant in agros aut mare Caspium
   vexant inaequales procellae
      usque, nec Armeniis in oris,

amice Valgi, stat glacies iners 5
mensis per omnis aut Aquilonibus
   querqueta Gargani laborant
      et foliis viduantur orni:

tu semper urges flebilibus modis
Mysten ademptum, nec tibi Vespero   10
   surgente decedunt amores
     nec rapidum fugiente solem.

at non ter aevo functus amabilem
ploravit omnis Antilochum senex
   annos, nec impubem parentes   15
     Troilon aut Phrygiae sorores

flevere semper. desine mollium
tandem querelarum, et potius nova
   cantemus Augusti tropaea
     Caesaris et rigidum Niphaten,   20

Medumque flumen gentibus additum
victis minores volvere vertices,
   intraque praescriptum Gelonos
     exiguis equitare campis.

                         Horace, *Odes* II. 9

7. *Garganus*: a mountain in Apulia.
14. *Antilochus*: son of Nestor (= *senex*) slain by Memnon.
16. *Troilus*: slain by Achilles.
20. *Niphates*: a mountain of Armenia.
21. *Medum flumen*: i.e. the Euphrates.

1 What is the burden of Horace's advice to Valgius? Do you
    find what he says unsympathetic and cruel?
2 Explain the structure of the poem. Which stanza, if any,
    stands out on its own? Can you suggest a reason why?
    What words in stanza 2 point the way to stanza 3?
3 What impression, if any, does the succession of the place-
    names (vv. 1–8) and changing scenes convey to the reader?
    Is there any logic behind the order of the scenes, and place-
    names? Or is it merely a random series?
4 Quinn (*Latin Explorations* 160) suggests *ademptum* (v. 10)
    may mean that Mystes has been taken away not by death,
    but by a rich lover. What would your verdict be, taking
    into account the whole tone of the poem, especially
    Horace's advice to Valgius?

5 Williams (*Tradition and Originality in Roman Poetry*) says: 'this ode...like many others moves in a circle so that the end echoes the beginning'. What does he mean?

6 How do you interpret vv. 17–end? Is Horace seriously asking Valgius to dry his tears and turn to patriotic poetry? If not, what *is* he suggesting?

(Compare *Odes* I. 33 addressed to Albius – generally taken as Tibullus – on a similar theme.)

27   *Two comparisons*

(A) CAESAR COMPARED WITH ANTONY

A bitter denouncement of Antony by Cicero in his *Second Philippic*.

Fuit in illo ingenium, ratio, memoria, litterae, cura, cogitatio, diligentia; res bello gesserat, quamvis rei publicae calamitosas, at tamen magnas; multos annos regnare meditatus, magno labore, magnis periculis quod cogitarat effecerat; muneribus, monumentis, congiariis, epulis multi-   5 tudinem imperitam delenierat; suos praemiis, adversarios clementiae specie devinxerat. quid multa? attulerat iam liberae civitati partim metu partim patientia consuetudinem serviendi. cum illo ego te dominandi cupiditate conferre possum, ceteris vero rebus nullo modo comparandus es.   10 sed ex plurimis malis quae ab illo rei publicae sunt inusta hoc tamen boni est quod didicit iam populus Romanus quantum cuique crederet, quibus se committeret, a quibus caveret. haec non cogitas, neque intellegis satis esse viris fortibus didicisse quam sit re pulchrum, beneficio gratum,   15 fama gloriosum tyrannum occidere? an, cum illum homines non tulerint, te ferent? certatim posthac, mihi crede, ad hoc opus curretur neque occasionis tarditas exspectabitur.

Cicero, *Philippicae* II. 116–17

1 Compare the list of qualities Cicero attributes to Caesar with those he attributes to Antony – what does this tell us about his attitudes to each of them?

2 What, in a nutshell, is Cicero saying?

3 What exactly are Cicero's criticisms of Antony in this passage? How can Cicero exonerate Caesar from much the same censure?

4 What kind of things had Caesar done which Cicero might consider *rei publicae calamitosas* (ll. 2–3)?

5 Explain sentence 4 (ll. 11–14). Is Cicero being sarcastic?

6 To what is Cicero referring in sentence 5 (ll. 14–16)?

7 Comment on the stylistic effects. What devices does Cicero employ in order to make his comparison stark and clear-cut? What other evidence of careful composition does this passage afford?

8 Read the whole piece aloud several times. Is the rhythm agreeable? In the lengthy lists of qualities and deeds, how does Cicero vary the length of his cola to effect? Is the tendency to amplify (i.e. do the members tend to become increasingly long), or to diminish, or is there a mixture of the two?

9 How often, and where in particular, does Cicero make an emphasis by repetition? Is it effective?

(B) A COMPARISON OF CAESAR AND THE YOUNGER CATO

Memoria mea ingenti virtute, divorsis moribus fuere viri duo, M. Cato et C. Caesar. quos quoniam res obtulerat, silentio praeterire non fuit consilium, quin utriusque naturam et mores, quantum ingenio possum, aperirem. igitur iis genus aetas eloquentia prope aequalia fuere, 5 magnitudo animi par, item gloria, sed alia alii. Caesar beneficiis ac munificentia magnus habebatur, integritate vitae Cato. ille mansuetudine et misericordia clarus factus, huic severitas dignitatem addiderat. Caesar dando sublevando ignoscundo, Cato nihil largiundo, gloriam adeptus 10 est. in altero miseris perfugium erat, in altero malis pernicies. illius facilitas, huius constantia laudabatur. postremo Caesar in animum induxerat laborare, vigilare; negotiis amicorum intentus sua neglegere, nihil denegare quod dono dignum esset; sibi magnum imperium, exer- 15 citum, bellum novom exoptabat, ubi virtus enitescere posset. at Catoni studium modestiae, decoris, sed maxume

severitatis erat; non divitiis cum divite neque factione cum
factioso, sed cum strenuo virtute, cum modesto pudore,
cum innocente abstinentia certabat; esse quam videri bonus   20
malebat: ita, quo minus petebat gloriam, eo magis illum
adsequebatur.   Sallust, *Bellum Catilinae* LIII. 6 – LIV

1 Sallust says complimentary things about both men, but
   whom does he prefer, and from what do you infer this?
   Of whom has he more to say, and why? List the qualities
   attributed to each; which particular qualities do you think
   appealed to Sallust? Try to give reasons for your choice.
   How far does sentence 9 (ll. 13–17) make your decision as
   to which man Sallust preferred a clear-cut one?
2 What device(s) does Sallust use to make his comparison
   effective?
3 Is the writing *clear*? Is the reader ever in doubt as to who
   is being described?
4 What picture of Cato does Sallust draw? (Look up Cato
   in a Classical dictionary.) How does what Cato says, and the
   way he says it, suit the nature of the historical man himself?

(A) AND (B)

1 How does the basic purpose of (B) differ from that of (A)?
2 How far does Sallust's judgement on Caesar correspond to,
   and differ from, that of Cicero? Could you account for this?
3 How does the *structure* of the two comparisons differ?
   Which is the easier method of composition?
4 How does the difference of structure affect the kind of style?
   Taking into account the fact that Cicero was writing a speech
   and Sallust was writing history, whose language is more
   elaborate, whose easier to read? Could you have guessed that
   (A) was from a speech and (B) was from a history? If so, how?

28 *A spoonful of sugar*

Lucretius explains his reasons for writing philosophy in verse.

Nunc age quod superest cognosce et clarius audi.
nec me animi fallit quam sint obscura; sed acri
percussit thyrso laudis spes magna meum cor

et simul incussit suavem mi in pectus amorem
musarum, quo nunc instinctus mente vigenti   5
avia Pieridum peragro loca nullius ante
trita solo. iuvat integros accedere fontis
atque haurire, iuvatque novos decerpere flores
insignemque meo capiti petere inde coronam
unde prius nulli velarint tempora musae;   10
primum quod magnis doceo de rebus et artis
religionum animum nodis exsolvere pergo,
deinde quod obscura de re tam lucida pango
carmina, musaeo contingens cuncta lepore.
id quoque enim non ab nulla ratione videtur;   15
sed veluti pueris absinthia taetra medentes
cum dare conantur, prius oras pocula circum
contingunt mellis dulci flavoque liquore,
ut puerorum aetas improvida ludificetur
labrorum tenus, interea perpotet amarum   20
absinthi laticem deceptaque non capiatur,
sed potius tali pacto recreata valescat,
sic ego nunc, quoniam haec ratio plerumque videtur
tristior esse quibus non est tractata, retroque
vulgus abhorret ab hac, volui tibi suaviloquenti   25
carmine Pierio rationem exponere nostram
et quasi musaeo dulci contingere melle,
si tibi forte animum tali ratione tenere
versibus in nostris possem, dum perspicis omnem
naturam rerum qua constet compta figura.   30

Lucretius, *De Rerum Natura* I. 921–50

1   Lucretius is explaining his reasons for propounding
    philosophy in verse. What do they amount to? Can you
    think of any other reasons he might have had which he
    does not mention?
2   To what does *thyrso* refer in v. 3? Why does Lucretius use
    this metaphor?
3   Lucretius mentions in this passage his greatest purpose in
    writing *De Rerum Natura*. Where?
4   Where does the simile begin and end? Is it apt? (Do
    you detect a pun?) How far does its application extend?
    Does Lucretius mean to imply that his philosophy thus

presented will have the same effect as the honeyed medicine
does on the boy (v. 21), i.e. that the reader will be taken in,
but all for his own good? – or does the application of the
simile fall down here? Can you think of a modern English
metaphor apart from that suggested by the title given
above which embraces the same idea as Lucretius' simile?

5 *dum* in v. 29 is variously translated as 'while' and 'until'
('idiomatic pres. indic.' Bailey). Which is the better
translation and why?

6 Bailey calls these 'exquisite verses'. Do you agree? Is any
part of them what you would term beautiful?

7 Can you think of any other philosophy – of any sort –
which has been written in verse? Is such an undertaking
doomed to failure? Does Lucretius seem to put philosophy first, or poetry? Consider vv. 11–15. Some critics
have labelled Lucretius as a poet who wrote about philosophy. On the evidence of this passage alone, have they
got it the right way round?

29 *How they brought the news...*

(A)

Ἑσπέρα μὲν γὰρ ἦν, ἧκε δ᾽ ἀγγέλλων τις ὡς τοὺς πρυτάνεις
ὡς Ἐλάτεια κατείληπται. καὶ μετὰ ταῦθ᾽ οἱ μὲν εὐθὺς
ἐξαναστάντες μεταξὺ δειπνοῦντες, τούς τ᾽ ἐκ τῶν σκηνῶν
τῶν κατὰ τὴν ἀγορὰν ἐξεῖργον καὶ τὰ γέρρ᾽ ἀνεπετάννυσαν, οἱ δὲ τοὺς στρατηγοὺς μετεπέμποντο καὶ τὸν   5
σαλπικτὴν ἐκάλουν· καὶ θορύβου πλήρης ἦν ἡ πόλις. τῇ
δ᾽ ὑστεραίᾳ, ἅμα τῇ ἡμέρᾳ, οἱ μὲν πρυτάνεις τὴν βουλὴν
ἐκάλουν εἰς τὸ βουλευτήριον, ὑμεῖς δ᾽ εἰς τὴν ἐκκλησίαν
ἐπορεύεσθε, καὶ πρὶν ἐκείνην χρηματίσαι καὶ προβουλεῦσαι,
πᾶς ὁ δῆμος ἄνω καθῆτο. καὶ μετὰ ταῦθ᾽ ὡς ἦλθεν ἡ βουλὴ 10
καὶ ἀπήγγειλαν οἱ πρυτάνεις τὰ προσηγγελμέν᾽ ἑαυτοῖς καὶ
τὸν ἥκοντα παρήγαγον κἀκεῖνος εἶπεν, ἠρώτα μὲν ὁ κῆρυξ
'τίς ἀγορεύειν βούλεται;' παρήει δ᾽ οὐδείς. πολλάκις δὲ
τοῦ κήρυκος ἐρωτῶντος, οὐδὲν μᾶλλον ἀνίστατ᾽ οὐδείς,
ἁπάντων μὲν τῶν στρατηγῶν παρόντων, ἁπάντων δὲ   15
τῶν ῥητόρων, καλούσης δὲ τῆς πατρίδος τῇ κοινῇ φωνῇ
τὸν ἐροῦνθ᾽ ὑπὲρ σωτηρίας· ἦν γὰρ ὁ κῆρυξ κατὰ τοὺς

νόμους φωνὴν ἀφίησι, ταύτην κοινὴν τῆς πατρίδος δίκαιον ἡγεῖσθαι.

4–5. ἀνεπετάννυσαν: i.e. 'unfolded the hurdles', though the manuscripts have ἐνεπίμπρασαν, 'burnt the hurdles'. The meaning has not been satisfactorily determined, but this must be some reference either to clearing space or to sending signals.

1 Comment on the sequence of subjects and tenses of verbs and participles in each sentence. What effect does the continual change produce?
2 Trace the course of the narrative. Does the writer keep strictly to the facts all the time? If he elaborates, say where and suggest why.
3 In what emotional state do you feel the people were at that time? Is the human reaction studied in depth?
4 Point out any *specifically* rhetorical devices. What do you feel the writer's purpose was in depicting the episode like this?

(B)

Ἐς δὲ τὰς Ἀθήνας ἐπειδὴ ἠγγέλθη, ἐπὶ πολὺ μὲν ἠπίστουν καὶ τοῖς πάνυ τῶν στρατιωτῶν ἐξ αὐτοῦ τοῦ ἔργου δια-πεφευγόσι καὶ σαφῶς ἀγγέλλουσι, μὴ οὕτω γε ἄγαν πανσυδὶ διεφθάρθαι· ἐπειδὴ δὲ ἔγνωσαν, χαλεποὶ μὲν ἦσαν τοῖς ξυμπροθυμηθεῖσι τῶν ῥητόρων τὸν ἔκπλουν, ὥσπερ οὐκ 5 αὐτοὶ ψηφισάμενοι, ὠργίζοντο δὲ καὶ τοῖς χρησμολόγοις τε καὶ μάντεσι καὶ ὁπόσοι τι τότε αὐτοὺς θειάσαντες ἐπήλ-πισαν ὡς λήψονται Σικελίαν. πάντα δὲ πανταχόθεν αὐτοὺς ἐλύπει τε καὶ περιειστήκει ἐπὶ τῷ γεγενημένῳ φόβος τε καὶ κατάπληξις μεγίστη δή. 10

1 Where does this writer concentrate his attention?
2 How effective do you find his description of the people's reactions?
3 Whose account is more forbidding, whose more directly descriptive?
4 Whose account reads more fluently? Illustrate your answer.
5 Assign each piece, with reasons, to an author.

30 *The story of Narcissus*

Fons erat inlimis, nitidis argenteus undis,
quem neque pastores neque pastae monte capellae
contigerant aliudve pecus, quem nulla volucris
nec fera turbarat nec lapsus ab arbore ramus;
gramen erat circa, quod proximus umor alebat,   5
silvaque sole locum passura tepescere nullo.
hic puer et studio venandi lassus et aestu
procubuit faciemque loci fontemque secutus,
dumque sitim sedare cupit, sitis altera crevit,
dumque bibit, visae conreptus imagine formae   10
spem sine corpore amat, corpus putat esse, quod
                                              unda est.
adstupet ipse sibi vultuque inmotus eodem
haeret ut e Pario formatum marmore signum.
spectat humi positus geminum, sua lumina, sidus
et dignos Baccho, dignos et Apolline crines   15
inpubesque genas et eburnea colla decusque
oris et in niveo mixtum candore ruborem
cunctaque miratur, quibus est mirabilis ipse.
se cupit inprudens et, qui probat, ipse probatur,
dumque petit, petitur pariterque accendit et ardet.   20
inrita fallaci quotiens dedit oscula fonti!
in mediis quotiens visum captantia collum
bracchia mersit aquis nec se deprendit in illis!
quid videat, nescit, sed, quod videt, uritur illo
atque oculos idem, qui decipit, incitat error.   25
credule, quid frustra simulacra fugacia captas?
quod petis, est nusquam; quod amas, avertere, perdes!
ista repercussae, quam cernis, imaginis umbra est:
nil habet ista sui: tecum venitque manetque,
tecum discedet, si tu discedere possis.   30

Ovid, *Metamorphoses* III. 407–36

1 Verses 1–7: what reasons could there be why Ovid spends
   so much time describing the pool to which Narcissus
   comes? Are the details of this description at all symbolic –
   or is this a case of embellishment for its own sake?

2 How vividly does Ovid's setting of the scene spring to the imagination? How does he achieve the effect of clarity?

3 Comment on the sound of v. 6, and the word order of v. 21.

4 What quality characterises this passage – wit, emotion, sarcasm, romance, drama? How would you describe the poet's viewpoint? Is he sympathetic – or utterly detached – or does he change about? Comment on vv. 26–30: do they alter or confirm your view?

5 What is the poet's attitude to Narcissus? How does he portray the youth? Is he a psychologically mixed-up boy, or a universal symbol of self-love?

6 Examine closely vv. 9–11 and vv. 18–20; what facet of Ovid's art do they represent? How do you regard such phenomena? How successful is L. P. Wilkinson's translation of these lines:

(9–11)   And as he drank, smitten by what did seem
         A face, he loved an unsubstantial dream,
         And what was shadow mere, did substance deem.

(18–20) What's admirable in himself admires,
         Approves himself, fondly himself desires,
         Seeking is sought, and burns with self-made fires.

Where else do we see Ovid revelling in this strange situation?

7 How effective is the word order of vv. 14–15, and the enjambement of vv. 14–17? What effect is achieved?

8 What effect does the apostrophe to Narcissus (vv. 26–30) have on the narrative?

9 Examine the use of tense in this passage. Would a repeated perfect tense have been (*a*) as easy to put into the verse from a metrical point of view, (*b*) equally satisfactory from the point of view of the narrative? Comment on the force of the change of tense (v. 21).

10 'Tempted by the paradoxes inherent in the situation, Ovid...pursues his idea too far' (Wilkinson, *Ovid Recalled* 435). What is meant by this remark? Do you agree?

11 Wilkinson continues: 'Milton borrows some details, but refines by transforming or omitting others.'

> (Eve) 'I thither went
> With unexperienced thought, and laid me down
> On the green bank, to look into the clear,
> Smooth lake, that to me seemed another sky.
> As I bent down to look, just opposite,
> A shape within the watery gleam appeared
> Bending to look on me. I started back,
> It started back, but pleased I soon returned,
> Pleased it returned as soon with answering looks
> Of sympathy and love. There had I fixed
> Mine eyes till now, and pined with vain desire,
> Had not a voice thus warned me: "What thou seest,
> What there thou seest, fair creature, is thyself:
> With thee it came and goes."'
>
> Milton, *Paradise Lost* IV. 456–69.

How much did Milton borrow? Is Wilkinson right in his criticism?

12 In the light of your observations, what claim do you think Ovid's poetry has to being 'great poetry'? Or do you think it a mere exercise in verbal acrobatics? Or something between the two? Where are the logodaedalics most tortuous? Is the charm of the scene ruined by this? If not, how is it saved?

31 *Slaughter at the Assinarus*

Νικίας δ' ἐπειδὴ ἡμέρα ἐγένετο ἦγε τὴν στρατιάν· οἱ δὲ
Συρακόσιοι καὶ οἱ ξύμμαχοι προσέκειντο τὸν αὐτὸν τρόπον
πανταχόθεν βάλλοντές τε καὶ κατακοντίζοντες. καὶ οἱ
Ἀθηναῖοι ἠπείγοντο πρὸς τὸν Ἀσσίναρον ποταμόν, ἅμα
μὲν βιαζόμενοι ὑπὸ τῆς πανταχόθεν προσβολῆς ἱππέων τε   5
πολλῶν καὶ τοῦ ἄλλου ὄχλου, οἰόμενοι ῥᾷόν τι σφίσιν
ἔσεσθαι, ἢν διαβῶσι τὸν ποταμόν, ἅμα δ' ὑπὸ τῆς ταλαι-
πωρίας καὶ τοῦ πιεῖν ἐπιθυμίᾳ. ὡς δὲ γίγνονται ἐπ' αὐτῷ,
ἐσπίπτουσιν οὐδενὶ κόσμῳ ἔτι, ἀλλὰ πᾶς τέ τις διαβῆναι
αὐτὸς πρῶτος βουλόμενος καὶ οἱ πολέμιοι ἐπικείμενοι χαλε-   10

πὴν ἤδη τὴν διάβασιν ἐποίουν· ἀθρόοι γὰρ ἀναγκαζόμενοι
χωρεῖν ἐπέπιπτόν τε ἀλλήλοις καὶ κατεπάτουν, περί τε τοῖς
δορατίοις καὶ σκεύεσιν οἱ μὲν εὐθὺς διεφθείροντο, οἱ δὲ
ἐμπαλασσόμενοι κατέρρεον. ἐς τὰ ἐπὶ θάτερά τε τοῦ ποτα-
μοῦ παραστάντες οἱ Συρακόσιοι (ἦν δὲ κρημνῶδες) ἔβαλλον 15
ἄνωθεν τοὺς Ἀθηναίους, πίνοντάς τε τοὺς πολλοὺς ἀσμέ-
νους καὶ ἐν κοίλῳ ὄντι τῷ ποταμῷ ἐν σφίσιν αὐτοῖς ταρασ-
σομένους. οἵ τε Πελοποννήσιοι ἐπικαταβάντες τοὺς ἐν τῷ
ποταμῷ μάλιστα ἔσφαζον. καὶ τὸ ὕδωρ εὐθὺς διέφθαρτο,
ἀλλ᾽ οὐδὲν ἧσσον ἐπίνετό τε ὁμοῦ τῷ πηλῷ ἡματωμένον 20
καὶ περιμάχητον ἦν τοῖς πολλοῖς.   Thucydides VII. 84

1 Examine each sentence and say where it advances the
   narrative, where it adds colour to the events. Outside the
   strict narrative, where does Thucydides' interest seem to lie?
2 Which tense of verb is most frequently used, and why?
   Explain any exceptions.
3 Note the position of all participles in relation to their main
   verbs; could you distinguish 'verbal' from 'adjectival'
   participles on these grounds?
4 How do the following phrases help you to picture the
   scene more acutely? τὸν αὐτὸν τρόπον (l. 2); οὐδενὶ
   κόσμῳ (l. 9); ἤδη (l. 11); κατέρρεον (l. 14).
5 Thucydides says very little about the Athenians, yet a
   strong impression comes across. How? What words imply
   their feelings? Do you feel Thucydides to be impartial to
   their fate?

32   The defeat and death of Catiline

Sed ubi omnibus rebus exploratis Petreius tuba signum dat,
cohortis paulatim incedere iubet; idem facit hostium exercitus. postquam eo ventum est, unde a ferentariis proelium
conmitti posset, maxumo clamore eum infestis signis con-
currunt; pila omittunt, gladiis res geritur. veterani pristinae 5
virtutis memores comminus acriter instare, illi haud timidi
resistunt: maxuma vi certatur. interea Catilina cum expe-
ditis in prima acie vorsari, laborantibus succurrere, integros
pro sauciis arcessere, omnia providere, multum ipse pugnare,

44

saepe hostem ferire: strenui militis et boni imperatoris officia 10
simul exequebatur. Petreius ubi videt Catilinam, contra ac
ratus erat, magna vi tendere, cohortem praetoriam in medios
hostis inducit eosque perturbatos atque alios alibi resistentis
interficit. deinde utrimque ex lateribus ceteros adgreditur.
Manlius et Faesulanus in primis pugnantes cadunt. Catilina 15
postquam fusas copias seque cum paucis relicuom videt,
memor generis atque pristinae suae dignitatis in confer-
tissumos hostis incurrit ibique pugnans confoditur.

Sed confecto proelio, tum vero cerneres, quanta audacia
quantaque animi vis fuisset in exercitu Catilinae. nam fere 20
quem quisque pugnando locum ceperat, eum amissa anima
corpore tegebat. pauci autem, quos medios cohors prae-
toria disiecerat, paulo divorsius, alis alibi stantes, sed omnes
tamen advorsis volneribus conciderant. Catilina vero longe
a suis inter hostium cadavera repertus est, paululum etiam 25
spirans ferociamque animi, quam habuerat vivos, in voltu
retinens. postremo ex omni copia neque in proelio neque
in fuga quisquam civis ingenuos captus est: ita cuncti suae
hostiumque vitae iuxta pepercerant. neque tamen exercitus
populi Romani laetam aut incruentam victoriam adeptus 30
erat. nam strenuissumus quisque aut occiderat in proelio
aut graviter volneratus discesserat. multi autem, qui e
castris visundi aut spoliandi gratia processerant, volventes
hostilia cadavera amicum alii, pars hospitem aut cognatum
reperiebant; fuere item qui inimicos suos cognoscerent. ita 35
varie per omnem exercitum laetitia, maeror, luctus atque
gaudia agitabantur.   Sallust, *Bellum Catilinae* LX–LXI

1 What general remarks would you make on the narrative
   style of Sallust in this passage? The following are quoted
   by Syme (*Sallust*, OUP 1964, 260ff.) as qualities of
   Sallust's style: the use of plain and simple phrases to
   achieve powerful effects; love of destroying the 'harmony'
   of periods; abnormal grammar; 'poetic' usages. Try to
   list examples of all these phenomena from this passage, and
   add any other features you think worthy of note.
2 What is your impression of the feeling of this piece? Which
   of the following adjectives best describes the language:
   emotive, restrained, rhetorical, economical, poetic?

3 Quintilian talks of Sallust's *immortalis velocitas*. Can you see what he meant by this? Illustrate your answer.

4 Of Thucydides, Quintilian said: *densus et brevis, et semper instans sibi*. Could the same judgement be applied to Sallust in any degree?

5 Examine the rhythm of this passage. How many short periods are there? Are they used to effect?

6 Does the author pay much attention to *structure*, or does the evidence point rather to the contrary?

7 What is Sallust's attitude in describing this episode? Can we learn anything of his character from this?

8 Quintilian said that Livy was 'better for school children', but that Sallust was the 'greater historian'. What is there in Sallust's writing that might have impressed Quintilian so greatly?

33 *Facit indignatio versum*

Juvenal is forced to write satire by a sense of moral indignation at the sorry state of Rome.

Cur tamen hoc potius libeat decurrere campo,
per quem magnus equos Auruncae flexit alumnus,
si vacat ac placidi rationem admittitis, edam.
  Cum tener uxorem ducat spado, Mevia Tuscum
figat aprum et nuda teneat venabula mamma,   5
patricios omnis opibus cum provocet unus
quo tondente gravis iuveni mihi barba sonabat,
cum pars Niliacae plebis, cum verna Canopi
Crispinus Tyrias umero revocante lacernas
ventilet aestivum digitis sudantibus aurum   10
nec sufferre queat maioris pondera gemmae,
difficile est saturam non scribere. nam quis iniquae
tam patiens urbis, tam ferreus, ut teneat se,
causidici nova cum veniat lectica Mathonis
plena ipso, post hunc magni delator amici   15
et cito rapturus de nobilitate comesa
quod superest, quem Massa timet, quem munere palpat
Carus et a trepido Thymele summissa Latino;

cum te summoveant qui testamenta merentur
noctibus, in caelum quos evehit optima summi   20
nunc via processus, vetulae vesica beatae?
unciolam Proculeius habet, sed Gillo deuncem,
partes quisque suas ad mensuram inguinis heres.
accipiat sane mercedem sanguinis et sic
palleat ut nudis pressit qui calcibus anguem   25
aut Lugudunensem rhetor dicturus ad aram.
quid referam quanta siccum iecur ardeat ira,
cum populum gregibus comitum premit hic spoliator
pupilli prostantis et hic damnatus inani
iudicio? quid enim salvis infamia nummis?   30
exul ab octava Marius bibit et fruitur dis
iratis, at tu victrix, provincia, ploras.

Juvenal, Satire I. 19–50

1 What *feeling* characterises this passage?
2 Divide this piece into sense-blocks. Do they fit neatly
  together, or are the transitions rather staccato? Juvenal is
  famous for his *vignettes*; does he use detail effectively
  here?
3 What is the effect of the repeated *cum . . . cum*, leading up to
  the main clause in v. 12?
4 Examine carefully vv. 5–12 and break the passage down
  into sense-elements. What comment would you make
  about the structure here?
5 The four kinds of people Juvenal is sneering at fall into
  two groups; what are they?
6 Do you see the author as a bitter and jealous man, or a
  highly moral character? Would Juvenal have shouted so
  loudly if he had himself been wealthy?
7 On what grounds could Juvenal's style be called rhetorical?
8 Give examples of the way Juvenal uses word order and
  position within the line to underline a point he is making.
9 This passage could be relevant (*mutatis mutandis*) to
  twentieth-century London life. Write a translation in
  modern English making the appropriate changes to bring
  it up to date.

34 *A bull fight*

The chief danger to the strength of bulls and horses is the excess of the passion of love. This can cause great rivalries between them.

> Sed non ulla magis viris industria firmat
> quam Venerem et caeci stimulos avertere amoris,
> sive boum sive est cui gratior usus equorum.
> atque ideo tauros procul atque in sola relegant
> pascua post montem oppositum et trans flumina lata,   5
> aut intus clausos satura ad praesepia servant.
> carpit enim viris paulatim uritque videndo
> femina, nec nemorum patitur meminisse nec herbae
> dulcibus illa quidem inlecebris, et saepe superbos
> cornibus inter se subigit decernere amantis.   10
> pascitur in magna Sila formosa iuvenca:
> illi alternantes multa vi proelia miscent
> vulneribus crebris; lavit ater corpora sanguis,
> versaque in obnixos urgentur cornua vasto
> cum gemitu; reboant silvaeque et longus Olympus.   15
> nec mos bellantis una stabulare, sed alter
> victus abit longeque ignotis exsulat oris,
> multa gemens ignominiam plagasque superbi
> victoris, tum quos amisit inultus amores,
> et stabula aspectans regnis excessit avitis.   20

> Virgil, *Georgics* III. 209–28

1 Look up *relego* (v. 4). What kind of image is Virgil using? Is it effective?
2 Translate vv. 7–8: whose *viris*?
3 Give examples of effective word-positioning in vv. 8 and 11. Are these examples of the same kind, and of a similar purpose, or not?
4 There is a strong contrast between vv. 11 and 12. What is it, and how is it contrived?
5 What do you notice about the language of vv. 12–20, if anything? and the language of the imagery of vv. 16ff.?

6 Is Virgil talking throughout merely of the animal kingdom, or has he in mind the male and female of the human species?

35 *All is vanity*

Τίς κεν αἰνήσειε νόῳ πίσυνος Λίνδου ναέταν Κλεόβουλον,
ἀενάοις ποταμοῖσ᾽ ἄνθεσί τ᾽ εἰαρινοῖς
ἀελίου τε φλογὶ χρυσέας τε σελάνας
καὶ θαλασσαίαισι δίναισ᾽ ἀντία θέντα μένος στάλας;
ἅπαντα γάρ ἐστι θεῶν ἥσσω· λίθον δὲ   5
καὶ βρότεοι παλάμαι θραύοντι· μωροῦ
φωτὸς ἅδε βουλά.

Simonides, *Poetae Melici Graeci* (Page) 581

1. *Cleobulus* was tyrant of Rhodes *c.* 600 B.C.
6. θραύοντι = θραύουσι.

1 Analyse the steps in the argument of the poem.
2 Discuss the effect in the first sentence of (*a*) the last four words, especially their position and scansion, and (*b*) the five elements mentioned. (Why mention ἀενάοις ποταμοῖσ᾽ and ἄνθεσί τ᾽ εἰαρινοῖς?)
3 Compare the length of the last three sentences with the first sentence. What effect does this produce?
4 Why is the fourth sentence so effectively final?
5 Learn the poem by heart.
6 Compare this poem with Shelley's 'Ozymandias' in tone and purpose.

Ozymandius

I met a traveller from an antique land
Who said: Two vast and trunkless legs of stone
Stand in the desert. . . Near them, on the sand,
Half sunk, a shattered visage lies, whose frown,
And wrinkled lip, and sneer of cold command,   5
Tell that its sculptor well those passions read
Which yet survive, stamped on these lifeless things,
The hand that mocked them and the heart that fed:
And on the pedestal these words appear:
'My name is Ozymandias, king of kings: 10

Look on my works, ye Mighty, and despair!'
Nothing beside remains. Round the decay
Of that colossal wreck, boundless and bare
The lone and level sands stretch far away.

P. B. Shelley

hand = sculptor's hand.   mocked = imitated.
heart = king's heart.

36   *The destruction of Alba*

'One of the greatest disasters that can befall man: the destruction of a city. A city is the outward sum of man's nobility; in it his condition is most thoroughly humanized.' (G. Steiner, *Language and Silence*.)

Inter haec iam praemissi Albam erant equites qui multitudinem traducerent Romam. legiones deinde ductae ad diruendam urbem. quae ubi intravere portas, non quidem fuit tumultus ille nec pavor qualis captarum esse urbium solet, cum effractis portis stratisve ariete muris aut arce vi 5
capta clamor hostilis et cursus per urbem armatorum omnia ferro flammaque miscet; sed silentium triste ac tacita maestitia ita defixit omnium animos, ut prae metu obliti quid relinquerent, quid secum ferrent deficiente consilio rogitantesque alii alios, nunc in liminibus starent, nunc errabundi 10
domos suas ultimum illud visuri pervagarentur. ut vero iam equitum clamor exire iubentium instabat, iam fragor tectorum quae diruebantur ultimis urbis partibus audiebatur pulvisque ex distantibus locis ortus velut nube inducta omnia impleverat, raptim quibus quisque poterat elatis, cum larem 15
ac penates tectaque in quibus natus quisque educatusque esset relinquentes exirent, iam continens agmen migrantium impleverat vias, et conspectus aliorum mutua miseratione integrabat lacrimas, vocesque etiam miserabiles exaudiebantur, mulierum praecipue, cum obsessa ab armatis 20
templa augusta praeterirent ac velut captos relinquerent deos. egressis urbe Albanis Romanus passim publica privataque omnia tecta adaequat solo, unaque hora quadringentorum annorum opus quibus Alba steterat excidio ac

ruinis dedit. templis tamen deum – ita enim edictum ab 25
rege fuerat – temperatum est.

Roma interim crescit Albae ruinis.   Livy 1. 29

1 On what does Livy concentrate his description? Is it the
   destruction itself of Alba?
2 What overwhelming impression about the people of Alba
   emerges from this description, and what are the key-
   words which point it?
3 Does Livy sympathise with the people? If so, how does he
   justify Rome's destruction of Alba?
4 In sentence 3 (ll. 3–7) what purpose is served by going
   into such detail about the normal course of events in
   sacking a city?
5 Does sentence 5 (ll. 11–22) contradict what Livy has said
   in sentence 4 (ll. 7–11)? What stylistic device in sentence 4
   helps Livy depict the helplessness of the people?
6 What is the point of the clause *cum . . . exirent* in sentence 5
   (ll. 15–17)? Is it of any importance to the narrative?
7 In view of your answers to the above questions, would you
   conclude that Livy paid great attention to the structure and
   composition of his history? Is he what you would term a
   'stylist'?

37   *Piety unrewarded*

Siqua recordanti benefacta priora voluptas
    est homini, cum se cogitat esse pium,
nec sanctam violasse fidem, nec foedere nullo
    divum ad fallendos numine abusum homines,
multa parata manent in longa aetate, Catulle,   5
    ex hoc ingrato gaudia amore tibi.
nam quaecumque homines bene cuiquam aut dicere possunt
    aut facere, haec a te dictaque factaque sunt.
omnia quae ingratae perierunt credita menti.
    quare iam te cur amplius excrucies?   10
quin tu animo offirmas atque istinc teque reducis,
    et dis invitis desinis esse miser?
difficile est longum subito deponere amorem,
    difficile est, verum hoc qua lubet efficias:

una salus haec est, hoc est tibi pervincendum,   15
    hoc facias, sive id non pote sive pote.
o di, si vestrum est misereri, aut si quibus umquam
    extremam iam ipsa in morte tulistis opem,
me miserum aspicite et, si vitam puriter egi,
    eripite hanc pestem perniciemque mihi,   20
quae mihi subrepens imos ut torpor in artus
    expulit ex omni pectore laetitias.
non iam illud quaero, contra me ut diligat illa,
    aut, quod non potis est, esse pudica velit:
ipse valere opto et taetrum hunc deponere morbum.   25
    o di, reddite mi hoc pro pietate mea.   Catullus LXXVI

1 The poem begins with a string of generalised remarks;
   reading between the lines, what do you think Catullus is
   talking about?
2 What impression do you receive of the mood of the poem?
   Would you call it bitter, angry, ironic, self-pitying, sad or
   resigned? Does the mood change at all in the course of the
   poem?
3 Explain the structure of the poem. How many blocks of
   sense are there? Are the transitions smooth or not?
4 How is the rhythm of v. 15 expressive of the poet's mood?
5 Consider the tone of Catullus' prayer; what force do his
   actual requests have in setting the mood of the poem? Is
   the general tone hopeful or hopeless?
6 *si vitam puriter egi* (v. 19)...*pro pietate mea* (v. 26). Is
   Catullus being priggish and self-righteous? If not, how
   should these words be explained?
7 How would you describe the *style* of the poem? Is it
   simple and unaffected, or inflated, 'learned', rhetorical,
   ornamental? Does it suit the subject matter?

38   *Inertia*

Ἦμος δὲ σκόλυμός τ' ἀνθεῖ καὶ ἠχέτα τέττιξ
δενδρέῳ ἐφεζόμενος λιγυρὴν καταχεύετ' ἀοιδὴν
πυκνὸν ὑπὸ πτερύγων, θέρεος καματώδεος ὥρῃ,
τῆμος πιότατί τ' αἶγες, καὶ οἶνος ἄριστος,

μαχλόταται δὲ γυναῖκες, ἀφαυρότατοι δέ τοι ἄνδρες   5
εἰσίν, ἐπεὶ κεφαλὴν καὶ γούνατα Σείριος ἄζει,
αὐαλέος δέ τε χρὼς ὑπὸ καύματος· ἀλλὰ τότ’ ἤδη
εἴη πετραίη τε σκιὴ καὶ βίβλινος οἶνος
μάζα τ’ ἀμολγαίη γάλα τ’ αἰγῶν σβεννυμενάων
καὶ βοὸς ὑλοφάγοιο κρέας μή πω τετοκυίης   10
πρωτογόνων τ’ ἐρίφων· ἐπὶ δ’ αἴθοπα πινέμεν οἶνον,
ἐν σκιῇ ἑζόμενον, κεκορημένον ἦτορ ἐδωδῆς,
ἀντίον ἀκραέος Ζεφύρου τρέψαντα πρόσωπα·
κρήνης δ’ ἀενάου καὶ ἀπορρύτου ἥ τ’ ἀθόλωτος
τρὶς ὕδατος προχέειν, τὸ δὲ τέτρατον ἱέμεν οἴνου.   15

Hesiod, *Works and Days* 582–96

1 Summarise the thought that links the two sections of this
   passage.
2 In vv. 1–7, distinguish the signs of the season from its effects.
   How powerful do you find Hesiod’s description of the heat?
3 How does the emphasis change in vv. 7–15? Comment on
   the purpose of the intrusion of the Zephyr at v. 13.
4 Do you think that Hesiod dwells too extensively on any
   topics? Explain the reason for your answer.
5 This passage comes in the middle of a rather austere work,
   devoted to telling the farmer how to arrange his yearly round.
   Do you think this passage is serious, or simply a pleasant
   dream?
6 Say what you mean by a paratactic style of writing. How
   does this passage illustrate the virtues of such a style?

39   *Pro Rhodiensibus*

This is an extract from a speech of Cato, who is speaking in
the senate on behalf of the people of Rhodes. The year is
168 B.C. The extract is interesting not so much for its subject
matter as for the impression it gives us of the great Roman
who wrote and spoke it.

Scio solere plerisque hominibus rebus secundis atque pro-
lixis atque prosperis animum excellere atque superbiam
atque ferociam augescere atque crescere. quo mihi nunc

magnae curae est, quod haec res tam secunde processit, ne
quid in consulendo advorsi eveniat, quod nostras secundas 5
res confutet, neve haec laetitia nimis luxuriose eveniat.
advorsae res edomant et edocent, quid opus siet facto;
secundae res laetitia transvorsum trudere solent a recte consulendo atque intellegendo. quo maiore opere dico suadeo-
que, uti haec res aliquot dies proferatur, dum ex tanto 10
gaudio in potestatem nostram redeamus.

Atque ego quidem arbitror, Rhodienses noluisse nos ita
depugnare uti depugnatum est, neque regem Persen vinci.
sed non Rhodienses modo id noluere, sed multos populos
atque multas nationes idem noluisse arbitror. atque haud 15
scio an partim eorum fuerint qui non nostrae contumeliae
causa id noluerint evenire: sed enim id metuere ne, si
nemo esset homo quem vereremur, quidquid luberet face-
remus. ne sub imperio nostro in servitute nostra essent,
libertatis suae causa in ea sententia fuisse arbitror. atque 20
Rhodienses tamen Persen publice numquam adiuvere.
cogitate, quanto nos inter nos privatim cautius facimus.
nam unusquisque nostrum, si quis adversus rem suam quid
fieri arbitratur, summa vi contra nititur ne advorsus eam
fiat; quod illi tamen perpessi. 25

Cato, preserved in Gellius VI. 3. 14 and 16

1 Cato was renowned as an effective orator. Do you consider
   this successful oratory? What is Cato's mood? Describe
   the general impression it conveys.
2 Is this extract artistically composed – or rough-and-ready?
   What are the qualities of Cato's style?
3 Gellius, who is quoting this passage, said 'All that could
   perhaps have been expressed more elegantly and rhythmic-
   ally, but I do not think it could have been expressed more
   forcibly or vividly'. Discuss this assessment, and put
   forward your own, illustrating your answer with the
   appropriate parts of the speech.
4 Wilkinson (*Golden Latin Artistry* 180) quotes eleven types
   of inelegance in this extract, which later Roman rhetoricians
   would certainly have avoided. Make a list of the obvious
   ones. Do you find them offensive?
5 The best orators, we are told, avoided ugly sounds and
   lilting rhythms in their prose. Does Cato observe this 'rule'?

40 Hector and Andromache

Ὣς εἰπὼν οὗ παιδὸς ὀρέξατο φαίδιμος Ἕκτωρ·
ἂψ δ' ὁ πάϊς πρὸς κόλπον ἐϋζώνοιο τιθήνης
ἐκλίνθη ἰάχων, πατρὸς φίλου ὄψιν ἀτυχθείς,
ταρβήσας χαλκόν τε ἰδὲ λόφον ἱππιοχαίτην,
δεινὸν ἀπ' ἀκροτάτης κόρυθος νεύοντα νοήσας.   5
ἐκ δὲ γέλασσε πατήρ τε φίλος καὶ πότνια μήτηρ·
αὐτίκ' ἀπὸ κρατὸς κόρυθ' εἵλετο φαίδιμος Ἕκτωρ,
καὶ τὴν μὲν κατέθηκεν ἐπὶ χθονὶ παμφανόωσαν·
αὐτὰρ ὅ γ' ὃν φίλον υἱὸν ἐπεὶ κύσε πῆλέ τε χερσίν,
εἶπε δ' ἐπευξάμενος Διί τ' ἄλλοισίν τε θεοῖσι·   10
'Ζεῦ ἄλλοι τε θεοί, δότε δὴ καὶ τόνδε γενέσθαι
παῖδ' ἐμόν, ὡς καὶ ἐγώ περ, ἀριπρεπέα Τρώεσσιν,
ὧδε βίην τ' ἀγαθόν, καὶ Ἰλίου ἶφι ἀνάσσειν·
καί ποτέ τις εἴποι "πατρός γ' ὅδε πολλὸν ἀμείνων"
ἐκ πολέμου ἀνιόντα· φέροι δ' ἔναρα βροτόεντα   15
κτείνας δήϊον ἄνδρα, χαρείη δὲ φρένα μήτηρ.'
Ὣς εἰπὼν ἀλόχοιο φίλης ἐν χερσὶν ἔθηκε
παῖδ' ἑόν· ἡ δ' ἄρα μιν κηώδεϊ δέξατο κόλπῳ
δακρυόεν γελάσασα· πόσις δ' ἐλέησε νοήσας,
χειρί τέ μιν κατέρεξεν ἔπος τ' ἔφατ' ἔκ τ' ὀνόμαζε·   20
'δαιμονίη, μή μοί τι λίην ἀκαχίζεο θυμῷ·
οὐ γάρ τίς μ' ὑπὲρ αἶσαν ἀνὴρ Ἄϊδι προϊάψει·
μοῖραν δ' οὔ τινά φημι πεφυγμένον ἔμμεναι ἀνδρῶν,
οὐ κακόν, οὐδὲ μὲν ἐσθλόν, ἐπὴν τὰ πρῶτα γένηται.
ἀλλ' εἰς οἶκον ἰοῦσα τὰ σ' αὐτῆς ἔργα κόμιζε,   25
ἱστόν τ' ἠλακάτην τε, καὶ ἀμφιπόλοισι κέλευε
ἔργον ἐποίχεσθαι· πόλεμος δ' ἄνδρεσσι μελήσει
πᾶσι, μάλιστα δ' ἐμοί, τοὶ Ἰλίῳ ἐγγεγάασιν.'
Ὣς ἄρα φωνήσας κόρυθ' εἵλετο φαίδιμος Ἕκτωρ
ἵππουριν· ἄλοχος δὲ φίλη οἶκόνδε βεβήκει   30
ἐντροπαλιζομένη, θαλερὸν κατὰ δάκρυ χέουσα.

Homer, *Iliad* VI. 466–96

1 Would you say that Hector and Andromache were happy
together? Which lines appeal to you as demonstrative of a
deep affection?

2 What is Hector's philosophy of life? Does it clash with

his portrayal as a loving husband and father? Is he more a man of war than of peace?

3 What implications are there that Hector will not return from battle?

4 It is said that Homer has the ability to sum up a total experience in a few words. Can you see any examples of this ability here?

5 The subject matter is very emotional; would you say the same of Homer's handling of it? Does this passage gain or lose from this?

6 Compare and contrast the above treatment with Sophocles' at *Ajax* 545–59. Before committing suicide, Ajax addresses his son:

Αἴ. Αἶρ' αὐτόν, αἶρε δεῦρο· ταρβήσει γὰρ οὔ,
νεοσφαγῆ που τόνδε προσλεύσσων φόνον,
εἴπερ δικαίως ἔστ' ἐμὸς τὰ πατρόθεν.
ἀλλ' αὐτίκ' ὠμοῖς αὐτὸν ἐν νόμοις πατρὸς
δεῖ πωλοδαμνεῖν κἀξομοιοῦσθαι φύσιν.   5
ὦ παῖ, γένοιο πατρὸς εὐτυχέστερος,
τὰ δ' ἄλλ' ὁμοῖος· καὶ γένοι' ἂν οὐ κακός.
καίτοι σε καὶ νῦν τοῦτό γε ζηλοῦν ἔχω,
ὁθούνεκ' οὐδὲν τῶνδ' ἐπαισθάνῃ κακῶν.
ἐν τῷ φρονεῖν γὰρ μηδὲν ἥδιστος βίος,   10
ἕως τὸ χαίρειν καὶ τὸ λυπεῖσθαι μάθῃς.
ὅταν δ' ἵκῃ πρὸς τοῦτο, δεῖ σ' ὅπως πατρὸς
δείξεις ἐν ἐχθροῖς οἷος ἐξ οἵου 'τράφης.
τέως δὲ κούφοις πνεύμασιν βόσκου, νέαν
ψυχὴν ἀτάλλων, μητρὶ τῇδε χαρμονήν.   15

41 *A woman scorned*

Dido realises that Aeneas is preparing to leave her, and is torn with grief and anger.

At regina dolos (quis fallere possit amantem?)
praesensit, motusque excepit prima futuros
omnia tuta timens. eadem impia Fama furenti
detulit armari classem cursumque parari.

saevit inops animi totamque incensa per urbem   5
bacchatur, qualis commotis excita sacris
Thyias, ubi audito stimulant trieterica Baccho
orgia nocturnusque vocat clamore Cithaeron.
tandem his Aenean compellat vocibus ultro:
'dissimulare etiam sperasti, perfide, tantum   10
posse nefas tacitusque mea decedere terra?
nec te noster amor nec te data dextera quondam
nec moritura tenet crudeli funere Dido?
quin etiam hiberno moliris sidere classem
et mediis properas Aquilonibus ire per altum,   15
crudelis? quid, si non arva aliena domosque
ignotas peteres, et Troia antiqua maneret,
Troia per undosum peteretur classibus aequor?
mene fugis? per ego has lacrimas dextramque tuam te
(quando aliud mihi iam miserae nihil ipsa reliqui),   20
per conubia nostra, per inceptos hymenaeos,
si bene quid de te merui, fuit aut tibi quicquam
dulce meum, miserere domus labentis et istam,
oro, si quis adhuc precibus locus, exue mentem.'

Virgil, *Aeneid* IV. 296–319

1 What is the effect of the parenthesis in the first line?
2 Summarise what Dido says (vv. 10–end). Is her anger convincing?
3 What examples of pointed word-positioning are there in this passage?
4 What do you notice of interest in the rhythmical structure of Dido's speech? Read it through several times before attempting to answer.
5 How many times does Virgil allude to Dido's mental state? What do you infer from this?
6 What especially puts Dido in a pathetic light?
7 Is this a successful picture of a woman scorned? Is Virgil's psychology convincing? Where especially does the poetry have the ring of truth?

42 Cicero defends the claim to Roman citizenship of his client, Archias

Si quid est in me ingeni, iudices, quod sentio quam sit exi-
guum, aut si qua exercitatio dicendi, in qua me non infitior
mediocriter esse versatum, aut si huiusce rei ratio aliqua ab
optimarum artium studiis ac disciplina profecta, a qua ego
nullum confiteor aetatis meae tempus abhorruisse, earum 5
rerum omnium vel in primis hic A. Licinius fructum a me
repetere prope suo iure debet. nam quoad longissime potest
mens mea respicere spatium praeteriti temporis et pueritiae
memoriam recordari ultimam, inde usque repetens hunc
video mihi principem et ad suscipiendam et ad ingrediendam 10
rationem horum studiorum exstitisse. quod si haec vox huius
hortatu praeceptisque conformata non nullis aliquando saluti
fuit, a quo id accepimus quo ceteris opitulari et alios servare
possemus, huic profecto ipsi, quantum est situm in nobis, et
opem et salutem ferre debemus. ac ne quis a nobis hoc ita 15
dici forte miretur, quod alia quaedam in hoc facultas sit ingeni
neque haec dicendi ratio aut disciplina, ne nos quidem huic
uni studio penitus umquam dediti fuimus. etenim omnes artes
quae ad humanitatem pertinent habent quoddam commune
vinclum et quasi cognatione quadam inter se continentur. sed 20
ne cui vestrum mirum esse videatur, me in quaestione legi-
tima et in iudicio publico, cum res agatur apud praetorem
populi Romani, lectissimum virum, et apud severissimos
iudices, tanto conventu hominum ac frequentia hoc uti
genere dicendi quod non modo a consuetudine iudiciorum 25
verum etiam a forensi sermone abhorreat, quaeso a vobis ut
in hac causa mihi detis hanc veniam accommodatam huic reo,
vobis, quem ad modum spero, non molestam, ut me pro
summo poeta atque eruditissimo homine dicentem hoc con-
cursu hominum litteratissimorum, hac vestra humanitate, 30
hoc denique praetore exercente iudicium, patiamini de studiis
humanitatis ac litterarum paulo loqui liberius, et in eius modi
persona quae propter otium ac studium minime in iudiciis
periculisque tractata est uti prope novo quodam et inusitato
genere dicendi.   Cicero, *Pro Archia* I–II 35

1　Lord Brougham considered this speech 'exquisitely composed', and many critics would judge it as the best of
Cicero. Do these six sentences form a well-balanced and
effective opening? Or is it too elaborate for modern taste?

2　Summarise the bare sense of what Cicero is saying. Why
did he say it in the way he did, and not in the way you have
expressed it in your summary?

3　Each *si*-clause in the first sentence is qualified by a relative
clause. What effect has each? Explain why in each case.

4　Why, when the speech is entitled *Pro Archia*, and when
Cicero's client is plainly called *Archias*, does he refer to
him as *Aulus Licinius* (l. 6)?

5　Explain the effect of the qualifying phrases *quoddam...
quasi...quadam* (ll. 19–20) upon the rest of the sentence.

6　Read the passage through aloud. Which part of it demands
most of your powers of breath-control? Can you suggest
why?

7　How many instances of what Cicero himself called *artifex
stilus* (the artistic pen) can you find?

8　Put the whole piece into the kind of English a twentieth-
century barrister might use. What kind of things did
Cicero say which would not be included today?

43　*The blessings of Dionysus*

Agaue, in a state of Dionysiac madness, has killed and now
holds the head of her son Pentheus. She believes it to be a lion's
head. Her father Cadmus attempts to bring her to her senses.

Κα.　Φεῦ φεῦ· φρονήσασαι μὲν οἷ' ἐδράσατε
ἀλγήσετ' ἄλγος δεινόν· εἰ δὲ διὰ τέλους
ἐν τῷδ' ἀεὶ μενεῖτ' ἐν ᾧ καθέστατε,
οὐκ εὐτυχοῦσαι δόξετ' οὐχὶ δυστυχεῖν.

Αγ.　τί δ' οὐ καλῶς τῶνδ' ἢ τί λυπηρῶς ἔχει;　　　　5

Κα.　πρῶτον μὲν ἐς τόνδ' αἰθέρ' ὄμμα σὸν μέθες.

Αγ.　ἰδού· τί μοι τόνδ' ἐξυπεῖπας εἰσορᾶν;

Κα.　ἔθ' αὑτὸς ἤ σοι μεταβολὰς ἔχειν δοκεῖ;

Αγ.　λαμπρότερος ἢ πρὶν καὶ διειπετέστερος.

Κα.　τὸ δὲ πτοηθὲν τόδ' ἔτι σῇ ψυχῇ πάρα;　　　　10

Αγ. οὐκ οἶδα τοὖπος τοῦτο. γίγνομαι δέ πως
    ἔννους, μεταστᾰθεῖσα τῶν πάρος φρενῶν.
Κα. κλύοις ἂν οὖν τι κἀποκρίναι᾽ ἂν σαφῶς;
Αγ. ὡς ἐκλέλησμαί γ᾽ ἃ πάρος εἴπομεν, πάτερ.
Κα. ἐς ποῖον ἦλθες οἶκον ὑμεναίων μέτα;   15
Αγ. Σπαρτῷ μ᾽ ἔδωκας, ὡς λέγουσ᾽, Ἐχίονι.
Κα. τίς οὖν ἐν οἴκοις παῖς ἐγένετο σῷ πόσει;
Αγ. Πενθεύς, ἐμῇ τε καὶ πατρὸς κοινωνίᾳ.
Κα. τίνος πρόσωπον δῆτ᾽ ἐν ἀγκάλαις ἔχεις;
Αγ. λέοντος, ὥς γ᾽ ἔφασκον αἱ θηρώμεναι.   20
Κα. σκέψαι νυν ὀρθῶς· βραχὺς ὁ μόχθος εἰσιδεῖν.
Αγ. ἔα, τί λεύσσω; τί φέρομαι τόδ᾽ ἐν χεροῖν;
Κα. ἄθρησον αὐτὸ καὶ σαφέστερον μάθε.
Αγ. ὁρῶ μέγιστον ἄλγος ἡ τάλαιν᾽ ἐγώ.
Κα. μῶν σοι λέοντι φαίνεται προσεικέναι;   25
Αγ. οὔκ, ἀλλὰ Πενθέως ἡ τάλαιν᾽ ἔχω κάρα.
Κα. ᾠμωγμένον γε πρόσθεν ἢ σὲ γνωρίσαι.
Αγ. τίς ἔκτανέν νιν; — πῶς ἐμὰς ἦλθεν χέρας;
Κα. δύστην᾽ ἀλήθει᾽, ὡς ἐν οὐ καιρῷ πάρει.

                        Euripides, *Bacchae* 1259–87

1 What is the effect of the vowel sounds in vv. 1–2?
2 What is Agaue's state of mind to begin with (vv. 5, 7)?
3 How does Cadmus first attempt to bring her to her senses
   (vv. 6, 8)? Why does he only *suggest* change?
4 What change in direction from v. 6 does Cadmus' question
   take in v. 10?
5 What accompanies Agaue's change of mind, and why is
   this so effective (vv. 11, 14)?
6 What sort of questions, and why these, does Cadmus ask
   as soon as Agaue seems to be returning to sanity?
7 Why does Agaue take so long to give the true answer to
   the τίνος of Cadmus' question at v. 19?
8 What is the connotation of φέρομαι (v. 22)?
9 Stichomythia is a very difficult convention within which
   to write. Why? To what abuses would it be most readily
   open? Discuss how Euripides overcomes them here.
10 How would you, as a play producer, organise the acting
   of this passage? Pay special attention to the use of the
   pause for effect.

44 *Ariadne auf Naxos*

A picture seen embroidered on the bridal couch of Peleus and Thetis. (This is taken from one of the few longer poems of Catullus.)

> Namque fluentisono prospectans litore Diae,
> Thesea cedentem celeri cum classe tuetur
> indomitos in corde gerens Ariadna furores,
> necdum etiam sese quae visit visere credit,
> utpote fallaci quae tum primum excita somno   5
> desertam in sola miseram se cernat harena.
> immemor at iuvenis fugiens pellit vada remis,
> irrita ventosae linquens promissa procellae.
> quem procul ex alga maestis Minois ocellis,
> saxea ut effigies bacchantis, prospicit, eheu,   10
> prospicit et magnis curarum fluctuat undis,
> non flavo retinens subtilem vertice mitram,
> non contecta levi velatum pectus amictu,
> non tereti strophio lactentis vincta papillas,
> omnia quae toto delapsa e corpore passim   15
> ipsius ante pedes fluctus salis alludebant.
> sed neque tum mitrae neque tum fluitantis amictus
> illa vicem curans toto ex te pectore, Theseu,
> toto animo, tota pendebat perdita mente.

Catullus, LXIV 52–70

1 What impression does the reader receive from the sounds of the opening lines?

2 What is the force of *immemor* in v. 7? Does it imply absent-mindedness, lack of a sense of duty, treachery, or what?

3 Catullus might have finished v. 7 *festinat in altum* (for example). Would anything be lost if this were substituted for what is in the text? Imagine the scene as described by Catullus – read the verse aloud: what can you see?

4 Discuss the purpose and effect of the repetition in vv. 10–11.

5 Both *Ariadne* (v. 10) and *Dido* are compared to *bacchantes*: 'totamque incensa per urbem / *bacchatur*; qualis commotis

excita sacris / Thyias, ubi audito stimulant trieterica
Baccho / orgia, nocturnusque vocat clamore Cithaeron'
(*Aen.* IV. 300ff.). Is the simile apt in the case of a woman
deserted by her lover? What is the point of comparison?

6 Give an English approximation to the metaphor *fluctuat
undis* in v. 11.

7 What is the force behind the repeated *non...non...non* in
vv. 12–14? *Is* there a strong emphasis here, or not?

8 Verses 12–16 present a vivid and striking picture. Do they
serve to express anything deeper?

9 What feeling do the alliteration and assonance in the last
two lines convey?

10 Would you say Catullus, in this extract, relies a good deal
on rhetorical devices?

(B) ARIADNE AGAIN – OVID'S VERSION

Tempus erat, vitrea quo primum terra pruina
    spargitur et tectae fronde queruntur aves.
incertum vigilans, a somno languida, movi
    Thesea prensuras semisupina manus;
nullus erat. referoque manus iterumque retempto   5
    perque torum moveo bracchia; nullus erat.
excussere metus somnum; conterrita surgo,
    membraque sunt viduo praecipitata toro.
protinus adductis sonuerunt pectora palmis,
    utque erat e somno turbida, rapta coma est.   10
luna fuit; specto siquid nisi litora cernam;
    quod videant oculi, nil nisi litus habent.
nunc huc, nunc illuc, et utroque sine ordine, curro;
    alta puellares tardat harena pedes.
interea toto clamavi in litore 'Theseu';   15
    reddebant nomen concava saxa tuum,
et quotiens ego te, totiens locus ipse vocabat;
    ipse locus miserae ferre volebat opem.
mons fuit; apparent frutices in vertice rari;
    hinc scopulus raucis pendet adesus aquis.   20
ascendo (vires animus dabat) atque ita late
    aequora prospectu metior alta meo.

inde ego (nam ventis quoque sum crudelibus usa)
    vidi praecipiti carbasa tenta Noto.
aut vidi aut acie tamquam vidisse putarem   25
    frigidior glacie semianimisque fui.
nec languere diu patitur dolor; excitor illo,
    excitor et summa Thesea voce voco.
'quo fugis?' exclamo. 'scelerate revertere Theseu,
    flecte ratem. numerum non habet illa suum.'   30
                        Ovid, *Heroides* x. 7–36

(Cf. *Ars Amatoria* I. 535 ff., which begins where this leaves off:

'Iamque iterum tundens mollissima pectora palmis,
    perfidus ille abiit. quid mihi fiet?' ait.
'quid mihi fiet?' ait: sonuerunt cymbala toto
    litore, et attonita tympana pulsa manu.
excidit illa metu, rupitque novissima verba: 5
    nullus in exanimi corpore sanguis erat.)

1 What is the effect of *luna fuit* (v. 11) and *mons fuit* (v. 19)? What force do these short, sharp sentences have?

2 How is the echo felt in vv. 15 ff.?

3 Give some examples of effective repetition within either the couplet or the line. Where are they most cleverly employed?

4 Note the use of tenses. Is this successfully varied, or monotonous and repetitive?

5 Does Ovid successfully convey the idea of Ariadne's sudden solitude?

6 Discuss the feeling of this passage; is it romantic, sentimental, or what? Do we really sympathise with Ariadne or does the charm of the poetry derive from our admiration of Ovid's faultless elegiacs?

7 'How many touches there are which are fresh and true' (Wilkinson, *Ovid Recalled* 104). Which do you consider the most vivid and beautiful lines, and why?

8 Ovid's poetry has often been said to suffer from an excess of rhetoric. What rhetorical devices are in evidence in these lines? Do they hamper, or contribute towards, the flow of the narrative?

Compare these two accounts:

1 Which of these two accounts ((A) and (B)) is the more effective and moving? Would you call Ovid's poetry in any sense 'great' poetry? Does Catullus' account deserve that title?

2 'The Heroines are far more pathetic when they simply tell their story than when they utter strings of reproaches and arguments, regrets and lamentations' (Wilkinson). Do you agree? On the whole, does the story gain or lose by being told in the first person?

3 What kind of stories, other than the *Heroides*, have been told by means of *letters*? Can you name any other authors who have used this device? Comment on its advantages and disadvantages as a narrative method.

45   *Aeneas gazes on the dead Pallas*

Ipse caput nivei fultum Pallantis et ora
ut vidit levique patens in pectore vulnus
cuspidis Ausoniae, lacrimis ita fatur obortis:
'tene,' inquit 'miserande puer, cum laeta veniret,
invidit Fortuna mihi, ne regna videres   5
nostra neque ad sedes victor veherere paternas?
non haec Evandro de te promissa parenti
discedens dederam, cum me complexus euntem
mitteret in magnum imperium metuensque moneret
acris esse viros, cum dura proelia gente.   10
et nunc ille quidem spe multum captus inani
fors et vota facit cumulatque altaria donis,
nos iuvenem exanimum et nil iam caelestibus ullis
debentem vano maesti comitamur honore.
infelix, nati funus crudele videbis!   15
hi nostri reditus exspectatique triumphi?
haec mea magna fides? at non, Evandre, pudendis
vulneribus pulsum aspicies, nec sospite dirum
optabis nato funus pater. ei mihi quantum
praesidium, Ausonia, et quantum tu perdis, Iule!'   20
                              Virgil, *Aeneid* XI. 39–58

1   What is the mood of Aeneas' speech? What is his attitude
    as he addresses the dead Pallas? What words or lines in
    particular convey this impression?
2   What picture of Evander does Aeneas paint, and how?
3   Is Aeneas himself convinced by the cold comfort which he
    can give to Evander (vv. 17 ff.)?
4   What effect upon the force of *at non...pater* (vv. 17–19)
    does the outburst *ei mihi quantum...Iule!* have?
5   What do you imagine would be the main difficulties in this
    piece confronting a translator?

Compare the following translations:

(A)

But, when Aeneas view'd the grisly wound
Which Pallas in his manly bosom bore,
And the fair flesh distain'd with purple gore:
First, melting into tears, the pious man
Deplor'd so sad a sight, then thus began: 5
'Unhappy youth! when Fortune gave the rest
Of my full wishes, she refus'd the best!
She came; but brought not thee along, to bless
My longing eyes, and share in my success:
She grudged thy safe return, the triumphs due   10
To prosp'rous valour, in the public view.
Not thus I promised, when thy father lent
Thy needless succour with a sad consent;
Embrac'd me, parting from th'Etrurian land,
And sent me to possess a large command.   15
He warn'd and from his own experience told,
Our foes were warlike, disciplin'd, and bold,
And now, perhaps, in hopes of thy return,
Rich odours on his loaded altars burn;
While we, with vain officious pomp, prepare   20
To send him back his portion of the war,
A bloody, breathless body, which can owe
No farther debt, but to the powers below.
The wretched father, ere his race is run,
Shall view the funeral honours of his son!   25
These are my triumphs of the Latian war,

65

Fruits of my plighted faith and boasted care!
And yet, unhappy sire, thou shalt not see
A son whose death disgrac'd his ancestry;
Thou shalt not blush, old man, however griev'd: 30
Thy Pallas no dishonest wound receiv'd.
He died no death to make thee wish, too late,
Thou hadst not liv'd to see his shameful fate.
But what a champion has th'Ausonian coast,
And what a friend hast thou, Ascanius, lost!'   35

                                              Dryden

(B)

Aeneas gazed on the pillowed head of Pallas
And his snow-white countenance; and the gaping
                                              wound
Cleft in his marble breast by the Ausonian spear.
Tears started to his eyes and he began,
'Did Fortune envy you, poor luckless boy,   5
That she bereft me of you when she came
To me and smiled her favours, forbidding you
To see my kingdom or ride home in triumph
To see your father's home? Not such were the
                                              promises
I gave on your behalf when I left Evander   10
And he embraced me, speeding me on my way
To a great empire, and warned me anxiously
That we should find our enemies fierce, and fight
Grim battles with an obdurate race. And now
In the grip of hopeless hopes perhaps even now he is   15
                                              offering
Vows to the gods, heaping the altars with gifts,
While we with the vain office of our griefs
Dead-march with the dead boy who owes
No debt to heaven's powers; now or henceforward.
O wretched father to see with your own eyes   20
The agonising funeral of your son!
Is this the promised, this the returning triumph?
This, all my pledge was worth? Ah yet, Evander,
It is no coward you shall look upon
With despicable wounds – you shall not be   25

A father craving death for the dishonour
A living son has brought so safely home.
Italy, cry alas for the great defender
Lost to you now, and lost to you, Iulus!'

Patric Dickinson, 1961

1 What are the relative merits of these two translations?
  Which does least violence to the original?
2 Which version conveys more successfully the *pathos* of
  these lines? Which is more 'poetic'? Which more
  'modern'?
3 Comment on the metres employed. Which is more
  suitable? Take into account the following remarks of
  Patric Dickinson: 'I have used a "measure" which is
  certainly not as "stately" as blank verse might have been.
  I have used English rhythm which seems to approximate to
  the Latin rhythm, each in its own way. I have done so in
  order to keep what a translator can truly keep going, and
  that is the impulse of the narrative.'
4 Is every translation doomed to failure? What would the
  perfect translation be like? How far is translation itself an
  aid or obstacle to the appreciation of Latin verse?

PART THREE

46 *Odi et Amo...*

(A)

Lesbia mi dicit semper male nec tacet umquam
   de me: Lesbia me dispeream nisi amat.
quo signo? quia sunt totidem mea: deprecor illam
   assidue, verum dispeream nisi amo.

Catullus LXXV

(B)

Huc est mens deducta tua mea, Lesbia, culpa
   atque ita se officio perdidit ipsa suo,
ut iam nec bene velle queat tibi, si optima fias,
   nec desistere amare, omnia si facias.

Catullus XCII

1 What do these two epigrams have in common, and how do
   they differ? Consider the rhythm, feeling, style and theme.
2 Can you say that one is more *successful* than the other?
   Give your reasons.
3 Discuss the effect of the rhythms in each poem.
4 Do you consider that such poetry is worth serious attention? What are its merits? Would you describe it as
   sophisticated, witty and clever – or trifling, and dull, and
   of no significance to a twentieth-century reader? – or how
   would you describe it?
5 How much is the impact of the poetry increased by a
   knowledge of the poet's affair with Lesbia?

47 *A monster catch*

A fisherman of Picenum catches a turbot of monstrous size, and
takes it as a gift to the emperor Domitian at Alba, knowing full
well that it would not be wise to keep or to sell such a prize.

Cum iam semianimum laceraret Flavius orbem
ultimus et calvo serviret Roma Neroni,
incidit Hadriaci spatium admirabile rhombi
ante domum Veneris, quam Dorica sustinet Ancon,
implevitque sinus; neque enim minor haeserat illis   5
quos operit glacies Maeotica ruptaque tandem
solibus effundit torrentis ad ostia Ponti
desidia tardos et longo frigore pingues.
destinat hoc monstrum cumbae linique magister
pontifici summo. quis enim proponere talem   10
aut emere auderet, cum plena et litora multo
delatore forent? dispersi protinus algae
inquisitores agerent cum remige nudo,
non dubitaturi fugitivum dicere piscem
depastumque diu vivaria Caesaris, inde   15
elapsum veterem ad dominum debere reverti.
si quid Palfurio, si credimus Armillato,
quidquid conspicuum pulchrumque est aequore toto
res fisci est, ubicumque natat. donabitur ergo,
ne pereat. iam letifero cedente pruinis   20
autumno, iam quartanam sperantibus aegris,
stridebat deformis hiems praedamque recentem
servabat; tamen hic properat, velut urgueat auster.
utque lacus suberant, ubi quamquam diruta servat
ignem Troianum et Vestam colit Alba minorem,   25
obstitit intranti miratrix turba parumper.
ut cessit, facili patuerunt cardine valvae;
exclusi spectant admissa obsonia patres.
itur ad Atriden. tum Picens 'accipe' dixit
'privatis maiora focis. genialis agatur   30
iste dies. propera stomachum laxare sagina
et tua servatum consume in saecula rhombum.
ipse capi voluit.' quid apertius? et tamen illi
surgebant cristae. nihil est quod credere de se
non possit cum laudatur dis aequa potestas.   35

Juvenal IV. 37–71

1. *Flavius...ultimus*: i.e. Domitian.
4. *Ancon*: founded by Syracusan exiles, and thus *Dorica*. Venus had a temple there.
6. *glacies Maeotica*: i.e. Sea of Azov. When the ice broke up, the fish swam into the Pontus.

15. *vivaria*: wealthy Romans often had fishponds in their gardens.
17. *Palfurius* and *Armillatus* were two successful informers.
21. *quartanam* (sc. *febrem*): a fever between the attacks of which was an interval of two days. A mild form of fever.
23. *auster*: a warm wind, prevailing in autumn.
24. Domitian had a villa in Alba Longa.
29. *Picens*: (fisherman) of Picenum.
33. *illi*: i.e. Domitian.

1 What is Juvenal's attitude in describing this episode?
2 Summarise the narrative content, divesting it of all satirical comment on the action.
3 What is the fisherman's attitude to the turbot? What effect does the turbot have on (*a*) him, (*b*) Domitian's minions and (*c*) the people?
4 What impression do you receive of the emperor himself from this extract?
5 What is the style and feeling of vv. 29–33? Why is Juvenal writing in this way?
6 Describe the style of vv. 20–3 (*iam letifero... servabat*). What purpose does this serve in the context?
7 Would you say this incident was historically true? If not, what is the poet's purpose in relating it?

48 *Narrative style*

(A) THE DEATH OF MESSALINA

Interim Messalina Lucullianis in hortis prolatare vitam, componere preces, non nulla spe et aliquando ira: tantum inter extrema superbiae gerebat. ac ni caedem eius Narcissus properavisset, verterat pernicies in accusatorem. nam Claudius domum regressus et tempestivis epulis delenitus, 5 ubi vino incaluit, iri iubet nuntiarique miserae (hoc enim verbo usum ferunt) dicendam ad causam postera die adesset. quod ubi auditum et languescere ira, redire amor ac, si cunctarentur, propinqua nox et uxorii cubiculi memoria timebantur, prorumpit Narcissus denuntiatque centurioni- 10 bus et tribuno, qui aderat, exequi caedem: ita imperatorem iubere. custos et exactor e libertis Euodus datur; isque raptim in hortos praegressus repperit fusam humi, adsidente matre Lepida, quae florenti filiae haud concors supremis eius neces-

71

sitatibus ad miserationem evicta erat suadebatque ne percus- 15
sorem opperiretur: transisse vitam neque aliud quam morti
decus quaerendum. sed animo per libidines corrupto nihil
honestum inerat; lacrimaeque et questus inriti ducebantur,
cum impetu venientium pulsae fores adstititque tribunus
per silentium, at libertus increpans multis et servilibus 20
probris.

Tunc primum fortunam suam introspexit ferrumque
accepit, quod frustra iugulo aut pectori per trepidationem
admovens ictu tribuni transigitur. corpus matri concessum.
nuntiatumque Claudio epulanti perisse Messalinam, non 25
distincto sua an aliena manu. nec ille quaesivit, poposcitque
poculum et solita convivio celebravit. ne secutis quidem
diebus odii gaudii, irae tristitiae, ullius denique humani
adfectus signa dedit, non cum laetantis accusatores aspi-
ceret, non cum filios maerentis. iuvitque oblivionem eius 30
senatus censendo nomen et effigies privatis ac publicis locis
demovendas.   Tacitus, *Annals* XI. 37–8

Write a critical appraisal of the passage, taking into consideration style, emotional appeal and attitude.

(B) SYME

Sir Ronald Syme is one of the great Tacitean scholars. In 1939
he wrote *The Roman Revolution* – the story of the last years
of the Republic and the foundation of the Empire. Here is an
extract taken at random:

The Antonians Decidius, Ventidius and Canidius, all famed
for victory or defeat in the eastern lands, became the pro-
verbial trio among the *novi homines* of the Revolution.
Which was appropriate, given the rarity and non-Latin
termination of their family names; but the Antonians were 5
not the worst. Advancement unheard-of now smiled upon
the avid, the brutal and the unscrupulous; even youth
became a commendation, when possession of neither tra-
ditions nor property could dull the edge of action. From
the beginning, the faction of Octavianus invited those who 10
had nothing to lose from war and adventure, among the

'foundation-members' being Agrippa and Salvidienus Rufus. Octavianus himself had only recently passed his twentieth birthday; Agrippa's age was the same to a year. Salvidienus, the earliest and greatest of his marshals, of 15 origin no more distinguished than Agrippa, was his senior in years and military experience. His example showed that the holding of senatorial office was not an indispensable qualification for leading armies of Roman legions. But Salvidienus was not unique: foreigners or freed slaves 20 might compete with knights for military command in the wars of the Revolution.

The Republic had been abolished. Whatever the outcome of the armed struggle, it could never be restored. Despotism ruled, supported by violence and confiscation. 25 The best men were dead or proscribed. The Senate was packed with ruffians, the consulate, once the reward of civic virtue, now became the recompense of craft or crime. 'Non mos, non ius.' So might the period be described. But the Caesarians claimed a right and a duty that trans- 30 cended all else, the avenging of Caesar. *Pietas* prevailed, and out of the blood of Caesar the monarchy was born.

R. Syme, *The Roman Revolution*, pp. 200–1

1 How much do you think Syme's narrative style was influenced by that of Tacitus? List the qualities of style both writers share.
2 What in Syme's writing is positively *un*-Tacitean? What features of Tacitus' style are notably absent from Syme's writing?
3 How obvious is the attitude of Syme to his subject-matter? Is Tacitus (in the above extract) more or less subjective? Does this, in either case, in any way affect the appeal of the writing?

49 *One over the eight*

Apart from the dialogue, the narrative of this passage is in reported speech, since it is Apollodorus' account to a friend of what Aristodemus had told him. Socrates has just finished a speech on the nature of Eros before the assembled company, which includes the host, Agathon, and the comic playwright, Aristophanes.

Εἰπόντος δὲ ταῦτα τοῦ Σωκράτους τοὺς μὲν ἐπαινεῖν, τὸν δὲ Ἀριστοφάνη λέγειν τι ἐπιχειρεῖν, ὅτι ἐμνήσθη αὐτοῦ λέγων ὁ Σωκράτης περὶ τοῦ λόγου· καὶ ἐξαίφνης τὴν αὔλειον θύραν κρουομένην πολὺν ψόφον παρασχεῖν ὡς κωμαστῶν, καὶ αὐλητρίδος φωνὴν ἀκούειν. τὸν οὖν Ἀγάθωνα, 'παῖδες', 5 φάναι, 'οὐ σκέψεσθε; καὶ ἐὰν μέν τις τῶν ἐπιτηδείων ᾖ, καλεῖτε· εἰ δὲ μή, λέγετε ὅτι οὐ πίνομεν ἀλλ' ἀναπαυόμεθα ἤδη.'

Καὶ οὐ πολὺ ὕστερον Ἀλκιβιάδου τὴν φωνὴν ἀκούειν ἐν τῇ αὐλῇ σφόδρα μεθύοντος καὶ μέγα βοῶντος, ἐρωτῶντος ὅπου Ἀγάθων καὶ κελεύοντος ἄγειν παρ' Ἀγάθωνα. ἄγειν 10 οὖν αὐτὸν παρὰ σφᾶς τήν τε αὐλητρίδα ὑπολαβοῦσαν καὶ ἄλλους τινὰς τῶν ἀκολούθων, καὶ ἐπιστῆναι ἐπὶ τὰς θύρας ἐστεφανωμένον αὐτὸν κιττοῦ τέ τινι στεφάνῳ δασεῖ καὶ ἴων, καὶ ταινίας ἔχοντα ἐπὶ τῆς κεφαλῆς πάνυ πολλάς, καὶ εἰπεῖν· 'ἄνδρες, χαίρετε· μεθύοντα ἄνδρα πάνυ σφόδρα 15 δέξεσθε συμπότην, ἢ ἀπίωμεν ἀναδήσαντες μόνον Ἀγάθωνα, ἐφ' ᾧπερ ἤλθομεν; ἐγὼ γάρ τοι, φάναι, χθὲς μὲν οὐχ οἷός τ' ἐγενόμην ἀφικέσθαι, νῦν δὲ ἥκω ἐπὶ τῇ κεφαλῇ ἔχων τὰς ταινίας, ἵνα ἀπὸ τῆς ἐμῆς κεφαλῆς τὴν τοῦ σοφωτάτου καὶ καλλίστου κεφαλὴν ἀναδήσω. ἆρα καταγελάσε- 20 σθέ μου ὡς μεθύοντος; ἐγὼ δέ, κἂν ὑμεῖς γελᾶτε, ὅμως εὖ οἶδ' ὅτι ἀληθῆ λέγω. ἀλλά μοι λέγετε αὐτόθεν, ἐπὶ ῥητοῖς εἰσίω ἢ μή; συμπίεσθε ἢ οὔ;'

Πάντας οὖν ἀναθορυβῆσαι καὶ κελεύειν εἰσιέναι καὶ κατακλίνεσθαι, καὶ τὸν Ἀγάθωνα καλεῖν αὐτόν. καὶ τὸν ἰέναι 25 ἀγόμενον ὑπὸ τῶν ἀνθρώπων, καὶ περιαιρούμενον ἅμα τὰς ταινίας ὡς ἀναδήσοντα, ἐπίπροσθε τῶν ὀφθαλμῶν ἔχοντα οὐ κατιδεῖν τὸν Σωκράτη, ἀλλὰ καθίζεσθαι παρὰ τὸν Ἀγάθωνα ἐν μέσῳ Σωκράτους τε καὶ ἐκείνου· παραχωρῆσαι γὰρ τὸν Σωκράτη ὡς ἐκεῖνον καθίζειν. παρακαθεζόμενον δὲ 30 αὐτὸν ἀσπάζεσθαί τε τὸν Ἀγάθωνα καὶ ἀναδεῖν.

Plato, *Symposium* 212c4–213b2

1 How does Plato bring out the togetherness of the drinking fraternity?
2 How does the picture of Alcibiades unfold? Show how Plato develops the picture of the man after his immediate entry.

3 What details of Alcibiades' appearance seem to you to be most exactly observed?
4 Describe the reactions of the party to the noises at the door, and say what these tell us about (*a*) the party, (*b*) Alcibiades.
5 Plato is reckoned to be one of the great stylists of the Greek language. Could you give examples of this from this passage? Do you find that style and subject matter clash in any way?

50   *Bad weather — the farmer's ruin*

Quid tempestates autumni et sidera dicam,
atque, ubi iam breviorque dies et mollior aestas,
quae vigilanda viris? vel cum ruit imbriferum ver,
spicea iam campis cum messis inhorruit et cum
frumenta in viridi stipula lactentia turgent?   5
saepe ego, cum flavis messorem induceret arvis
agricola et fragili iam stringeret hordea culmo,
omnia ventorum concurrere proelia vidi,
quae gravidam late segetem ab radicibus imis
sublimem expulsam eruerent: ita turbine nigro   10
ferret hiems culmumque levem stipulasque volantis.
saepe etiam immensum caelo venit agmen aquarum
et foedam glomerant tempestatem imbribus atris
collectae ex alto nubes; ruit arduus aether
et pluvia ingenti sata laeta boumque labores   15
diluit; implentur fossae et cava flumina crescunt
cum sonitu fervetque fretis spirantibus aequor.
ipse pater media nimborum in nocte corusca
fulmina molitur dextra, quo maxima motu
terra tremit, fugere ferae et mortalia corda   20
per gentis humilis stravit pavor; ille flagranti
aut Atho aut Rhopoden aut alta Ceraunia telo
deicit; ingeminant Austri et densissimus imber;
nunc nemora ingenti vento, nunc litora plangunt.
hoc metuens caeli mensis et sidera serva,   25
frigida Saturni sese quo stella receptet,
quos ignis caelo Cyllenius erret in orbis.
in primis venerare deos, atque annua magnae

sacra refer Cereri laetis operatus in herbis
extremae sub casum hiemis, iam vere sereno.   30
tum pingues agni et tum mollissima vina,
tum somni dulces densaeque in montibus umbrae.

Virgil, Georgics I. 311–42

1 In v. 8 and v. 12 what metaphors does Virgil use to describe
   the advent of a storm? Is this image used elsewhere?
2 Examine the storm passages carefully and list details of
   alliteration and assonance; what effect do the ends of vv. 3
   and 4 have? What is the effect of the elision in v. 10?
   What rhythms predominate in vv. 12–14 and 14–17?
3 In vv. 18–21, what vowels predominate? What is the effect
   of the alliteration? What sounds in vv. 21–4 suggest
   lightning, thunder and rain?
4 How do vv. 31–2 express the idea of peace after the storm?
   Consider especially the rhythm.
5 The *Georgics* have been called a farmer's manual. What
   instructions are given in this passage? Is the above definition satisfactory in the light of it? Could you offer a
   better one?
6 What is the relationship sketched between god and man in
   this passage? What role does nature play in the relationship?

51 *The suitors' reckoning*

Read this extract through carefully, and make your own
translation:

Αὐτὰρ ὁ γυμνώθη ῥακέων πολύμητις Ὀδυσσεύς,
ἆλτο δ' ἐπὶ μέγαν οὐδόν, ἔχων βιὸν ἠδὲ φαρέτρην
ἰῶν ἐμπλείην, ταχέας δ' ἐκχεύατ' ὀϊστοὺς
αὐτοῦ πρόσθε ποδῶν, μετὰ δὲ μνηστῆρσιν ἔειπεν·
'οὗτος μὲν δὴ ἄεθλος ἀάατος ἐκτετέλεσται·   5
νῦν αὖτε σκοπὸν ἄλλον, ὃν οὔ πώ τις βάλεν ἀνήρ,
εἴσομαι, αἴ κε τύχωμι, πόρῃ δέ μοι εὖχος Ἀπόλλων.'
    Ἦ καὶ ἐπ' Ἀντινόῳ ἰθύνετο πικρὸν ὀϊστόν.
ἦ τοι ὁ καλὸν ἄλεισον ἀναιρήσεσθαι ἔμελλε,
χρύσεον ἄμφωτον, καὶ δὴ μετὰ χερσὶν ἐνώμα,   10

ὄφρα πίοι οἴνοιο· φόνος δέ οἱ οὐκ ἐνὶ θυμῷ
μέμβλετο· τίς κ᾽ οἴοιτο μετ᾽ ἀνδράσι δαιτυμόνεσσι
μοῦνον ἐνὶ πλεόνεσσι, καὶ εἰ μάλα καρτερὸς εἴη,
οἷ τεύξειν θάνατόν τε κακὸν καὶ κῆρα μέλαιναν;
τὸν δ᾽ Ὀδυσεὺς κατὰ λαιμὸν ἐπισχόμενος βάλεν ἰῷ,   15
ἀντικρὺ δ᾽ ἀπαλοῖο δι᾽ αὐχένος ἤλυθ᾽ ἀκωκή.
ἐκλίνθη δ᾽ ἑτέρωσε, δέπας δέ οἱ ἔκπεσε χειρὸς
βλημένου, αὐτίκα δ᾽ αὐλὸς ἀνὰ ῥῖνας παχὺς ἦλθεν
αἵματος ἀνδρομέοιο· θοῶς δ᾽ ἀπὸ εἷο τράπεζαν
ὦσε ποδὶ πλήξας, ἀπὸ δ᾽ εἴδατα χεῦεν ἔραζε·   20
σῖτός τε κρέα τ᾽ ὀπτὰ φορύνετο. τοὶ δ᾽ ὁμάδησαν
μνηστῆρες κατὰ δώμαθ᾽, ὅπως ἴδον ἄνδρα πεσόντα.

Homer, *Odyssey* XXII. 1–22

Compare the following translations:

(A)

Now shrugging off his rags the wiliest fighter of the islands
leapt and stood on the broad door-sill, his own bow in his
        hand.
He poured out at his feet a rain of arrows from the quiver
and spoke to the crowd:
    'So much for that. Your clean-cut game is over.   5
Now watch me hit a target that no man has hit before,
if I can make this shot. Help me, Apollo.'
He drew to his fist the cruel head of an arrow for Antinoos
just as the young man leaned to lift his beautiful drinking
        cup,
embossed, two handled, golden: the cup was in his
        fingers: 10
the wine was even at his lips: and did he dream of death?
How could he? In that revelry amid his throng of friends
who could imagine a single foe – though strong foe
        indeed –
could dare to bring death's pain on him, and darkness
        on his eyes?
Odysseus' arrow hit him under the chin   15
and punched up to the feathers through his throat.
Backward and down he went, letting the wine-cup fall
from his shocked hand. Like pipes his nostrils jetted

crimson runnels, a river of mortal red,
and one last kick upset his table   20
knocking the bread and meat to soak in dusty blood.
Now as they craned to see their champion where he lay
the suitors jostled in uproar down the hall.

R. Fitzgerald, 1961

(B)

Shedding his rags, the indomitable Odysseus leapt onto
the great threshold with his bow and his full quiver, and
poured out the winged arrows at his feet.

'That match is played and won!' he shouted to the
Suitors. 'Now for another target! No man has hit yet;   5
but with Apollo's help I'll try.' And with that he levelled
a deadly shaft straight at Antinous.

Antinous had just reached for his golden cup to take a
draught of wine, and the rich, two-handled beaker was
balanced in his hands. No thought of bloodshed had entered 10
his head. For who could guess, there in that festive company, that one man, however powerful he might be, would
bring calamity and death to him against such odds? Yet
Odysseus shot his bolt and struck him in the throat. The
point passed clean through the soft flesh of his neck.   15
Dropping the cup as he was hit, he lurched over to one
side. His life-blood gushed from his nostrils in a turbid
jet. His foot lashed out and kicked the table from him; the
food was scattered on the ground, and his bread and meat
were smeared with gore.   20

When the Suitors saw the man collapse, there was an
angry outcry in the hall.

E. V. Rieu (Penguin Books 1946)

(C)

Then Odysseus of many counsels stripped him of his rags
and leaped on to the great threshold with his bow and
quiver full of arrows, and poured forth all the swift shafts
there before his feet, and spake among the wooers:

'Lo, now is this terrible trial ended at last; and now I   5
will make for another mark, which never yet man has

78

smitten, if perchance I may strike it and Apollo grant me renown.'

With that he pointed the bitter arrow at Antinous. Now he was about raising to his lips a fair two-eared chalice of gold, 10 and behold, he was handling it to drink of the wine, and death was far from his thoughts. For who among men at feast would deem that one man amongst so many, how hardy soever he were, would bring on him foul death and black fate? But Odysseus aimed and smote him with the 15 arrow in the throat, and the point passed clean out through his delicate neck, and he fell back and the cup dropped from his hand as he was smitten, and at once through his nostrils there came up a thick jet of slain man's blood, and quickly he spurned the table from him with his foot, and 20 spilt the food on the ground, and the bread and the roast flesh were defiled. Then the wooers raised a clamour through the halls when they saw the man fallen...

S. H. Butcher and A. Lang, 1889

1 Discuss the merits of these translations, first the verse translation (A), then the prose translations (B) and (C).
2 Disregarding the differences of verse and prose, which translation would you select as (a) nearest in spirit to the original; (b) nearest the word of the original? Which translation is the best combination of (a) and (b)?
3 How do the prose-styles of (B) and (C) reflect differences of intention on the part of the authors?

(B) E. V. Rieu: 'This version of the *Odyssey* is, in its intention at any rate, a genuine translation, not a paraphrase nor a retold tale. At the same time, and within the rules I have set myself, I have done my best to make Homer easy reading for those who are unfamiliar with the Greek world.'

(C) Butcher and Lang: 'We have attempted to tell once more, in simple prose, the story of Odysseus. We have tried to transfer, not all the truth about the poem, but the historical truth, into English. In this process Homer must lose at least half his charm...It may be objected, that the employment of language which does not come spontaneously to the lips, is an affectation out of place in a version of the *Odyssey*. To this we may answer that the Greek Epic dialect, like the English of our Bible, was a thing of slow growth and composite nature, that it was never a spoken language, nor, except for certain poetical purposes, a written language. Thus the Biblical English seems as nearly analogous to the Epic Greek, as anything our tongue has to offer.'

Discuss these remarks. Do the authors succeed in their aims? In particular, does Rieu's 'modern translation' avoid the charge of being a paraphrase in this passage? What do Butcher and Lang mean by 'historical truth'?

4 Butcher and Lang remark: 'There can be then, it appears, no final English translation of Homer. In each there must be, in addition to what is Greek and eternal, the element of what is modern, personal, and fleeting.' Which translation contains least of the 'personal and fleeting' element?

5 Does the metre employed in the verse translation successfully convey the 'feeling' of Homer? What kind of English verse is best suited to translate the Greek Epic hexameter?

6 Argue the pros and cons of translating verse into verse, as opposed to prose.

52   *The Catilinarian conspiracy*

The conspirators are at last in custody. A debate is held in which their fate is to be decided. Caesar argues in favour of leniency, as opposed to the suggestion of Silanus who has proposed that they be put to death.

(A) CAESAR'S SPEECH

Nam si digna poena pro factis eorum reperitur, novom consilium adprobo; sin magnitudo sceleris omnium ingenia exuperat, his utendum censeo, quae legibus conparata sunt.
    Plerique eorum, qui ante me sententias dixerunt, conposite atque magnifice casum rei publicae miserati sunt. quae   5

belli saevitia esset, quae victis adciderent, enumeravere:
rapi virgines, pueros; divelli liberos a parentum conplexu;
matres familiarum pati quae victoribus conlubuissent;
fana atque domos spoliari; caedem, incendia fieri; postremo armis, cadaveribus, cruore atque luctu omnia con- 10
pleri. sed, per deos inmortalis, quo illa oratio pertinuit?
an uti vos infestos coniurationi faceret? scilicet, quem res
tanta et tam atrox non permovit, eum oratio adcendet. non
ita est, neque quoiquam mortalium iniuriae suae parvae
videntur, multi eas gravius aequo habuere. sed alia aliis 15
licentia est, patres conscripti. qui demissi in obscuro vitam
habent, si quid iracundia deliquere, pauci sciunt, fama
atque fortuna eorum pares sunt; qui magno imperio prae-
diti in excelso aetatem agunt, eorum facta cuncti mortales
novere. ita in maxuma fortuna minuma licentia est; neque 20
studere neque odisse, sed minume irasci decet; quae apud
alios iracundia dicitur, ea in imperio superbia atque crude-
litas appellatur. equidem ego sic existumo, patres conscripti,
omnis cruciatus minores quam facinora illorum esse.

Sallust, Bellum Catilinae LI. 8–15

1 Write a précis of Caesar's argument.
2 Note down all the abstracts used. What do they tell us of
   the author's viewpoint? What seems to have been his
   major interest?
3 What does Caesar's summary of the preceding speeches
   tell us about what he thinks of them – even before he
   passes comment? Give the key-words which betray his
   attitude.
4 Examine the third sentence in detail. What is the tone of
   the passage *quae belli saevitia esset...luctu omnia compleri*?
   How would you describe the style?
5 Does Sallust suit this speech to the character of Caesar? Or
   is it pure Sallust? State your reasons.

(B) CATO'S SPEECH

The action Caesar proposes is weak. The death penalty is
required. Cato is indignant: the conspirators, he says, must be
made an example of, for the good of the republic.

Sed, per deos inmortalis, vos ego appello, qui semper
domos, villas, signa, tabulas vostras pluris quam rem publicam fecistis: si ista, quoiuscumque modi sunt quae am-
plexamini, retinere, si voluptatibus vostris otium praebere
voltis, expergiscimini aliquando et capessite rem publicam. 5
non agitur de vectigalibus neque de sociorum iniuriis:
libertas et anima nostra in dubio est.

Saepenumero, patres conscripti, multa verba in hoc ordine
feci, saepe de luxuria atque avaritia nostrorum civium
questus sum, multosque mortalis ea causa advorsos habeo. 10
qui mihi atque animo meo nullius umquam delicti gratiam
fecissem, haut facile alterius lubidini male facta condonabam.
sed ea tametsi vos parvi pendebatis, tamen res publica firma
erat, opulentia neglegentiam tolerabat. nunc vero non id
agitur, bonisne an malis moribus vivamus, neque quantum 15
aut quam magnificum imperium populi Romani sit, sed haec,
quoiuscumque modi videntur, nostra an nobiscum una
hostium futura sint. hic mihi quisquam mansuetudinem et
misericordiam nominat. iam pridem equidem nos vera
vocabula rerum amisimus: quia bona aliena largiri liberalitas, 20
malarum rerum audacia fortitudo vocatur, eo res publica
in extremo sita est. sint sane, quoniam ita se mores habent,
liberales ex sociorum fortunis, sint misericordes in furibus
aerari: ne illi sanguinem nostrum largiantur et, dum paucis
sceleratis parcunt, bonos omnis perditum eant. 25

Sallust, *Bellum Catilinae* LII. 4–12

1 Summarise the speech.
2 Is the *style* different from that of Caesar's? What typifies
  the style? List the similarities.
3 Is what Cato says more cogent than what Caesar says? Does
  he appeal more to the emotions than Caesar? How much is
  this a conflict of character, of two different types of men?
4 Is there much evidence of symmetry, i.e. careful balancing
  of clauses? Or do the periods give the impression of
  spontaneity?
5 On the basis of your answers to the above questions, write
  a critical appreciation of both passages. Which argument
  seems to you more cogent? (Find out which prevailed.)

53   Sophocles' defence

Χο.　Εὐίππου, ξένε, τᾶσδε χώ-
ρας ἵκου τὰ κράτιστα γᾶς ἔπαυλα,
τὸν ἀργῆτα Κολωνόν, ἔνθ᾽
ἁ λίγεια μινύρεται
θαμίζουσα μάλιστ᾽ ἀη-　　　　　　5
δὼν χλωραῖς ὑπὸ βάσσαις,
τὸν οἰνωπὸν ἔχουσα κισ-
σὸν καὶ τὰν ἄβατον θεοῦ
φυλλάδα μυριόκαρπον ἀνάλιον
ἀνήνεμόν τε πάντων　　　　　　10
χειμώνων· ἵν᾽ ὁ βακχιώ-
τας ἀεὶ Διόνυσος ἐμβατεύει
θείαις ἀμφιπολῶν τιθήναις.

θάλλει δ᾽ οὐρανίας ὑπ᾽ ἄ-
χνας ὁ καλλίβοτρυς κατ᾽ ἦμαρ αἰεὶ　　15
νάρκισσος, μεγάλοιν θεοῖν
ἀρχαῖον στεφάνωμ᾽, ὅ τε
χρυσαυγὴς κρόκος· οὐδ᾽ ἄυ-
πνοι κρῆναι μινύθουσιν
Κηφισοῦ νομάδες ῥεέ-　　　　　　20
θρων, ἀλλ᾽ αἰὲν ἐπ᾽ ἤματι
ὠκυτόκος πεδίων ἐπινίσεται
ἀκηράτῳ σὺν ὄμβρῳ
στερνούχου χθονός· οὐδὲ Μου-
σᾶν χοροί νιν ἀπεστύγησαν, οὐδ᾽ αὖ　25
ἁ χρυσάνιος Ἀφροδίτα.

Sophocles, *Oedipus Coloneus* 668–93

Cicero tells us that Sophocles, when on trial for being weak in
the head and unable to manage his own affairs, quoted this
chorus in his own defence, and was acquitted. Compare the
merits of the following translations and say what each is
trying to achieve:

(A)

Stranger, in this land of goodly steeds thou hast come to
earth's fairest home, even to our white Colonus; where

83

the nightingale, a constant guest, trills her clear note in the covert of green glades, dwelling amid the wine-dark ivy and the god's inviolate bowers, rich in berries and fruit, unvisited by sun, unvexed by wind of any storm; where the reveller Dionysus ever walks the ground, companion of the nymphs that nursed him.

And, fed of heavenly dew, the narcissus blooms morn by morn with fair clusters, crown of the Great Goddesses from of yore; and the crocus blooms with golden beam. Nor fail the sleepless founts whence the waters of Cephisus wander, but each day with stainless tide he moveth over the plains of the land's swelling bosom, for the giving of quick increase; nor hath the Muses' quire abhorred this place, nor Aphrodite of the golden rein.   R. C. Jebb

(B)

The land of running horses, fair
Colonus takes a guest;
He shall not seek another home,
For this, in all the earth and air,
Is most secure and loveliest.   5

In the god's untrodden vale
Where leaves and berries throng,
And wine-dark ivy climbs the bough,
The sweet, sojourning nightingale
Murmurs all night long.   10

No sun nor wind may enter there
Nor the winter's rain;
But ever through the shadow goes
Dionysus reveler,
Immortal maenads in his train.   15

Here with drops of heaven's dews
At daybreak all the year,
The clusters of narcissus bloom,
Time-hallowed garlands for the brows
Of those great ladies whom we fear.   20

The crocus like a little sun
Blooms with its yellow ray;
The river's fountains are awake,
And his nomadic streams that run
Unthinned forever, and never stay;   25

But like perpetual lovers move
On the maternal land.
And here the choiring Muses come,
And the divinity of love
With the gold reins in her hand.   30
                              Robert Fitzgerald

(c)

Here in our white Colonus, stranger guest,
Of all earth's lovely lands the loveliest,
Fine horses breed, and leaf-enfolded vales
Are thronged with sweetly-singing nightingales,
Screened in deep arbours, ivy, dark as wine,   5
And tangled bowers of berry-clustered vine;
To whose dark avenues and windless courts
The Grape-god with his nursing-nymphs resorts.

Here, chosen crown of goddesses, the fair
Narcissus blooms, bathing his lustrous hair   10
In dews of morning; golden crocus gleams
Along Cephisus' slow meandering streams,
Whose fountains never fail; day after day,
His limpid waters wander on their way
To fill with ripeness of abundant birth   15
The swelling bosom of our buxom earth.

Here Aphrodite rides with golden reins;
The Muses here consort.   E. F. Watling

On the strength of what you have learnt, make your own
translation.

54 *Narrative Style*

Read carefully the following passages:

(A)

Sed elati spe celeris victoriae et hostium fuga et superiorum
temporum secundis proeliis, nihil adeo arduum sibi esse
existimaverunt quod non virtute consequi possent, neque
finem prius sequendi fecerunt quam muro oppidi portisque
appropinquarunt. tum vero ex omnibus urbis partibus orto 5
clamore, qui longius aberant repentino tumultu perterriti,
cum hostem intra portas esse existimarent, sese ex oppido
eiecerunt. matres familiae de muro vestem argentumque
iactabant, et pectore nudo prominentes passis manibus
obtestabantur Romanos ut sibi parcerent neu, sicut Avarici 10
fecissent, ne a mulieribus quidem atque infantibus abs-
tinerent: non nullae de muro per manus demissae sese militibus tradebant.

(B)

Haec meditantibus advenit proficiscendi hora expectatione
tristior. quippe intra vallum deformitas haud perinde nota-
bilis: detexit ignominiam campus et dies. revulsae impera-
torum imagines, inhonora signa, fulgentibus hinc inde
Gallorum vexillis; silens agmen et velut longae exequiae; 5
dux Claudius Sanctus effosso oculo dirus ore, ingenio
debilior. duplicatur flagitium, postquam desertis Bonnensi-
bus castris altera se legio miscuerat. et vulgata captarum
legionum fama cuncti qui paulo ante Romanorum nomen
horrebant, procurrentes ex agris tectisque et undique effusi 10
insolito spectaculo nimium fruebantur.

(C)

Interim omnibus, Romanis hostibusque, proelio intentis,
magna utrimque vi pro gloria atque imperio his illis pro
salute certantibus, repente a tergo signa canere; ac primo
mulieres et pueri, qui visum processerant, fugere, deinde
uti quisque muro proxumus erat, postremo cuncti, armati 5

inermesque. quod ubi adcidit, eo acrius Romani instare, fundere ac plerosque tantummodo sauciare, dein super occisorum corpora vadere, avidi gloriae certantes murum petere, neque quemquam omnium praeda morari.

1 After an examination of both style and content, try to assign these three passages to their authors.
2 Could you say with certainty that (A) could *not* be Tacitus or Livy?
3 Could you say with certainty that (B) is *not* Sallust? What features of (C) may be considered as major clues to the identity of the author?
4 Is (A) more like (B) than (C) is? Or the opposite? Illustrate your answer.

55 *The true king*

L. Annaeus Seneca was the tutor of Nero, and a barrister, senator, philosopher and writer. Apart from other literary works, nine tragedies have come down to us. These had a profound influence on later tragedy – especially the French dramatists and Shakespeare. This is part of a choral passage from the *Thyestes*. The lyric passages of Seneca's plays are generally thought to be the very best of his poetic endeavours, and of considerable literary merit.

(A)

Regem non faciunt opes,
non vestis Tyriae color,
non frontis nota regiae,
non auro nitidae fores:
rex est qui posuit metus   5
et diri mala pectoris;
quem non ambitio impotens
et numquam stabilis favor
vulgi praecipitis movet,
non quicquid fodit Occidens   10
aut unda Tagus aurea
claro devehit alveo,
non quicquid Libycis terit

fervens area messibus,
quem non concutiet cadens   15
obliqui via fulminis,
non Eurus rapiens mare
aut saevo rabidus freto
ventosi tumor Hadriae,
quem non lancea militis,   20
non strictus domuit chalybs,
qui tuto positus loco
infra se videt omnia
occurritque suo libens
fato, nec queritur mori.   25

Seneca, Thyestes 344–68

(B) Later:

Stet quicumque volet potens
aulae culmine lubrico:
me dulcis saturet quies;
obscuro positus loco
leni perfruar otio,   5
nullis nota Quiritibus
aetas per tacitum fluat.
sic cum transierint mei
nullo cum strepitu dies,
plebeius moriar senex.   10
illi mors gravis incubat
qui, notus nimis omnibus,
ignotus moritur sibi.   Thyestes 391–403

1 What feelings (briefly summarised) do these two passages
   express?
2 What is the force of the adjectives *impotens* ((A), v. 7),
   stabilis (v. 8) and *praecipitis* (v. 9)?
3 Consider vv. 10ff. in (A). Why does Seneca list names
   in this way? What effect does it produce?
4 Describe the *atmosphere* of the poetry. What feeling, if any,
   does the steadily-repeated rhythm impart to the words?
5 Look up L. Annaeus Seneca in the *Oxford Classical
   Dictionary*. Do his relations with Nero throw any light on
   the sentiment of (B)?

56 *An age of disasters*

Opus adgredior opimum casibus, atrox proeliis, discors
seditionibus, ipsa etiam pace saevum. quattuor principes
ferro interempti: trina bella civilia, plura externa ac plerumque permixta: prosperae in Oriente, adversae in Occidente
res: turbatum Illyricum, Galliae nutantes, perdomita   5
Britannia et statim omissa: coortae in nos Sarmatarum ac
Sueborum gentes, nobilitatus cladibus mutuis Dacus, mota
prope etiam Parthorum arma falsi Neronis ludibrio. iam
vero Italia novis cladibus vel post longam saeculorum
seriem repetitis adflicta. haustae aut obrutae urbes, fecun-   10
dissima Campaniae ora; et urbs incendiis vastata, consump-
tis antiquissimis delubris, ipso Capitolio civium manibus
incenso. pollutae caerimoniae, magna adulteria: plenum
exiliis mare, infecti caedibus scopuli. atrocius in urbe
saevitum: nobilitas, opes, omissi gestique honores pro   15
crimine et ob virtutes certissimum exitium. nec minus
praemia delatorum invisa quam scelera, cum alii sacerdotia
et consulatus ut spolia adepti, procurationes alii et interio-
rem potentiam, agerent verterent cuncta odio et terrore.
corrupti in dominos servi, in patronos liberti; et quibus   20
deerat inimicus per amicos oppressi.

Tacitus, Histories I. 2

1 Describe the style of this passage. Is this effective writing?
   How does Tacitus achieve his effects?
2 Examine the periodic structure. Could you say with
   confidence that this could not be the work of Livy,
   Caesar or Sallust?
3 Give examples of deliberate variation of word order.
   What, if anything, is achieved by this?
4 What do we gather of Tacitus' attitude from this passage?
5 Sallust is famed for *velocitas* – could the same quality be
   attributed to the author of this extract?

57   *The blessings of philosophy*

Suave, mari magno turbantibus aequora ventis,
e terra magnum alterius spectare laborem;
non quia vexari quemquamst iucunda voluptas,
sed quibus ipse malis careas quia cernere suave est.
suave etiam belli certamina magna tueri   5
per campos instructa tua sine parte pericli.
sed nil dulcius est, bene quam munita tenere
edita doctrina sapientum templa serena,
despicere unde queas alios passimque videre
errare atque viam palantis quaerere vitae,   10
certare ingenio, contendere nobilitate,
noctes atque dies niti praestante labore
ad summas emergere opes rerumque potiri.
o miseras hominum mentis, o pectora caeca!
qualibus in tenebris vitae quantisque periclis   15
degitur hoc aevi quodcumquest! nonne videre
nil aliud sibi naturam latrare, nisi utqui
corpore seiunctus dolor absit, mente fruatur
iucundo sensu cura semota metuque?
ergo corpoream ad naturam pauca videmus   20
esse opus omnino, quae demant cumque dolorem,
delicias quoque uti multas substernere possint.
gratius interdum neque natura ipsa requirit,
si non aurea sunt iuvenum simulacra per aedes
lampadas igniferas manibus retinentia dextris,   25
lumina nocturnis epulis ut suppeditentur,
nec domus argento fulget auroque renidet
nec citharae reboant laqueata aurataque templa,
cum tamen inter se prostrati in gramine molli
propter aquae rivum sub ramis arboris altae   30
non magnis opibus iucunde corpora curant,
praesertim cum tempestas arridet et anni
tempora conspergunt viridantis floribus herbas.
nec calidae citius decedunt corpore febres,
textilibus si in picturis ostroque rubenti   35
iacteris, quam si in plebeia veste cubandum est.

Lucretius, *De Rerum Natura* II. 1–36

90

1 What is the poet's attitude to his theme? How does he feel about his mission?

2 Summarise the argument stage by stage, pruning from it all illustrative material. Explain the structure of this passage. Where is the climax?

3 Explain *in tenebris* in v. 15. What effect has *quodcumque* in v. 16? What image is used in v. 17 which is suggested by *latrare*?

4 Explain the examples given in vv. 24–36; are they apt choices?

5 What feeling characterises this passage: a smug, holier-than-thou attitude, a calm proselytising zeal, or what? Is Lucretius really sorry for his fellow men, or merely demonstrating his own philosophical peace of mind?

6 What is the burden of the philosophy Lucretius is propounding? (Do you imagine that it appealed to his contemporaries?)

58 *The Gauls enter Rome*

Romae interim satis iam omnibus, ut in tali re, ad tuen-
dam arcem compositis, turba seniorum domos regressi ad-
ventum hostium obstinato ad mortem animo exspectabant.
qui eorum curules gesserant magistratus, ut in fortunae
pristinae honorumque aut virtutis insignibus morerentur, 5
quae augustissima vestis est tensas ducentibus triumphanti-
busve, ea vestiti medio aedium eburneis sellis sedere. sunt
qui M. Folio pontifice maximo praefante carmen devovisse
eos se pro patria Quiritibusque Romanis tradant. Galli et
quia interposita nocte a contentione pugnae remiserant 10
animos et quod nec in acie ancipiti usquam certaverant
proelio nec tum impetu aut vi capiebant urbem, sine ira,
sine ardore animorum ingressi postero die urbem patente
Collina porta in forum perveniunt, circumferentes oculos ad
templa deum arcemque solam belli speciem tenentem. inde, 15
modico relicto praesidio ne quis in dissipatos ex arce aut
Capitolio impetus fieret, dilapsi ad praedam vacuis occursu
hominum viis, pars in proxima quaeque tectorum agmine
ruunt, pars ultima, velut ea demum intacta et referta praeda,

petunt; inde rursus ipsa solitudine absterriti, ne qua fraus 20
hostilis vagos exciperet, in forum ac propinqua foro loca
conglobati redibant; ubi eos, plebis aedificiis obseratis, pa-
tentibus atriis principum, maior prope cunctatio tenebat
aperta quam clausa invadendi; adeo haud secus quam
venerabundi intuebantur in aedium vestibulis sedentes 25
viros, praeter ornatum habitumque humano augustiorem,
maiestate etiam quam voltus gravitasque oris prae se ferebat
simillimos dis. ad eos velut simulacra versi cum starent,
M. Papirius, unus ex iis, dicitur Gallo barbam suam, ut tum
omnibus promissa erat, permulcenti scipione eburneo in 30
caput incusso iram movisse, atque ab eo initium caedis
ortum, ceteros in sedibus suis trucidatos; post principum
caedem nulli deinde mortalium parci, diripi tecta, exhaustis
inici ignes.   Livy v. 41

1 How *dramatic* is this account? What particular touches are
   designed to add drama?
2 How does Livy describe the attitude of the Gauls who are
   occupying Rome? With what does he contrast this? Is it an
   effective contrast?
3 The episode of the slaughter of the senators is dealt with
   fairly summarily. Is this in itself effective, or does it derive
   its force from the lengthy preparation, or do you not think
   it is forceful at all?
4 What reason can Livy have had for mentioning the fact
   that a Gaul touched the praetor's beard? What effect upon
   the reader does this have? Why did Papirius strike the
   Gaul?
5 Discuss in detail the end of this passage. How successful is
   it as a piece of writing? (Are the infinitives at the end of
   the last sentence better interpreted as historic, or as
   governed by *dicitur*?)
6 What remarks would you make on the style of this
   passage? Quintilian refers to Livy's *lactea ubertas* in
   narration – can you see what he means? Illustrate your
   answer.

59 *Martial, a native of Spain, returns to his home in retirement*

Dum tu forsitan inquietus erras
clamosa, Iuvenalis, in Subura,
aut collem dominae teris Dianae;
dum per limina te potentiorum
sudatrix toga ventilat vagumque   5
maior Caelius et minor fatigant:
me multos repetita post Decembres
accepit mea rusticumque fecit
auro Bilbilis et superba ferro.
hic pigri colimus labore dulci   10
Boterdum Plateamque – Celtiberis
haec sunt nomina crassiora terris –:
ingenti fruor inproboque somno,
quem nec tertia saepe rumpit hora,
et totum mihi nunc repono, quidquid   15
ter denos vigilaveram per annos.
ignota est toga, sed datur petenti
rupta proxima vestis a cathedra.
surgentem focus excipit superba
vicini strue cultus iliceti,   20
multa vilica quem coronat olla.
venator sequitur, sed ille quem tu
secreta cupias habere silva;
dispensat pueris rogatque longos
levis ponere vilicus capillos,   25
sic me vivere, sic iuvat perire.   Martial XII. 18

24. *dispensat*: 'distributes rations to'.
25. *levis*: i.e. 'close-cropped'; *ponere*: 'cut'. The fashionable Romans had slaves with long, often elaborately-styled hair to wait on them at dinner etc. Martial's bailiff asks his master to have the slaves' hair cut in the old Roman fashion.

1 The poem presents a broad contrast – what kind of contrast? Explain the structure of the poem with this in mind.
2 Why choose *Subura* (v. 2)? What effect do the names *Bilbilis*, *Boterdus* and *Platea* have in their context?

3 What is the point of v. 18? What impression does it
  convey?
4 What do vv. 24–5 tell us about Martial the country-lover?
5 Does Martial successfully convey the sense of easy, lazy
  happiness in Spain? Does he make the reader envy him?
  (Is this the point of the poem?)
6 Does the poem do anything more than sing the praises of
  country life as opposed to that of the city? Is it, for
  example, witty?

60   *The dream of a shadow*

Ὁ δὲ καλόν τι νέον λαχὼν
ἀβρότατος ἔπι μεγάλας
ἐξ ἐλπίδος πέτεται
ὑποπτέροις ἀνορέαις, ἔχων
κρέσσονα πλούτου μέριμναν. ἐν δ' ὀλίγῳ βροτῶν   5
τὸ τερπνὸν αὔξεται· οὕτω δὲ καὶ πίτνει χαμαί,
ἀποτρόπῳ γνώμᾳ σεσεισμένον.

ἐπάμεροι· τί δέ τις; τί δ' οὔ τις; σκιᾶς ὄναρ
ἄνθρωπος. ἀλλ' ὅταν αἴγλα διόσδοτος ἔλθῃ,
λαμπρὸν φέγγος ἔπεστιν ἀνδρῶν καὶ μείλιχος αἰών.   10
Αἴγινα φίλα μᾶτερ, ἐλευθέρῳ στόλῳ
πόλιν τάνδε κόμιζε Δὶ καὶ κρέοντι σὺν Αἰακῷ
Πηλεῖ τε κἀγαθῷ Τελαμῶνι σύν τ' Ἀχιλλεῖ.
                              Pindar, *Pythian Ode* VIII. 88–100

(Pindar wrote poems, on commission, to celebrate victories
in the Games. He had close connections with many cities in
Greece, especially Thebes and Aegina, and it is to a hero of
Aegina, Aristomenes, that he dedicates this ode. The gods in
vv. 12–13 are Aeginetan heroes; the reference to ἐλευθέρῳ
στόλῳ (v. 11) is perhaps a jibe at the imperialistic leanings of
Athens, which at that time exercised considerable influence
over Aegina.)

1 Trace the development of thought in this passage.
2 Translate and comment on the effectiveness of the imagery

94

behind: ἀβρότατος...ἀνορέαις (vv. 2–4), ἀποτρόπῳ γνώμᾳ σεσεισμένον (v. 7), αἴγλα διόσδοτος (v. 9), λαμπρὸν φέγγος (v. 10).

3 Which seems to cause more 'difficulty' to the reader, the words or the constructions? How would you describe Pindar's style, and where would you say it is most successful in this passage?

4 Why mention the heroes of old in this context? Does this negate in any way what Pindar has been saying previously?

5 Of vv. 9–10, Kitto says: 'this complete fusion of the physical, the intellectual, the moral, the spiritual and the sensuous'. Refer this judgement to the two stanzas and say if you agree with it.

6 How far does the following translation succeed in capturing the spirit of Pindar's style?

But he that has won some new
splendour, in high pride
of hope rides the air
on the wings of his man's strength, and keeps
desire beyond his wealth. In brief space mortals'
delight is exalted, and thus again it drops to the ground,
shaken by a backward doom.

We are things of a day. What are we? What are we not?
    The shadow of a dream
is man, no more. But when the brightness comes and God
gives it
there is a shining of light on men and their life is sweet.
Aigina, dear mother, bring this city to haven
in free guise, by Zeus' aid and strong Aiakos',
Peleus and goodly Telamon aiding, and with Achilles.
                                        Richmond Lattimore

61 *Roman v. Barbarian*

Calgacus, a Caledonian chieftain, is on home ground, and has most of the odds in his favour. The Roman general Agricola has no knowledge of the terrain, and supplies are running low.

It is clear that the ensuing battle will be decisive. Each general addresses his men:

(A) CALGACUS

Quotiens causas belli et necessitatem nostram intueor, magnus mihi animus est hodiernum diem consensumque vestrum initium libertatis toti Britanniae fore: nam et universi coistis et servitutis expertes, et nullae ultra terrae ac ne mare quidem securum inminente nobis classe Romana. 5 ita proelium atque arma, quae fortibus honesta, eadem etiam ignavis tutissima sunt. priores pugnae, quibus adversus Romanos varia fortuna certatum est, spem ac subsidium in nostris manibus habebant, quia nobilissimi totius Britanniae eoque in ipsis penetralibus siti nec ulla servientium 10 litora aspicientes, oculos quoque a contactu dominationis inviolatos habebamus. nos terrarum ac libertatis extremos recessus ipse ac sinus famae in hunc diem defendit: nunc terminus Britanniae patet, atque omne ignotum pro magnifico est; sed nulla iam ultra gens, nihil nisi fluctus ac saxa, 15 et infestiores Romani, quorum superbiam frustra per obsequium ac modestiam effugias. raptores orbis, postquam cuncta vastantibus defuere terrae, mare scrutantur: si locuples hostis est, avari, si pauper, ambitiosi, quos non Oriens, non Occidens satiaverit: soli omnium opes atque 20 inopiam pari adfectu concupiscunt. auferre trucidare rapere falsis nominibus imperium, atque ubi solitudinem faciunt, pacem appellant.   Tacitus, *Agricola* xxx

1 Summarise the content of this section.
2 What language and ideas here are well suited to the character of a fierce Caledonian chieftain? Has Tacitus made an effort to make the words appropriate to the character?
3 How far is Calgacus' indictment of Roman imperialism an appeal to the emotions? What are his most telling accusations?
4 Most of this speech must be pure imagination on the part of Tacitus. How far is it the kind of speech a Calgacus might have made, and how much the kind of speech a Roman historian would expect him to have made?

5　What conclusions would you draw about Tacitus' qualities as a rhetorician and stylist, taking into account the fact that, although a Roman patriot, he was able to put the case of the barbarian so eloquently and vividly?

(B) AGRICOLA

Septimus annus est, commilitones, ex quo virtute et auspiciis imperii Romani, fide atque opera vestra Britanniam vicistis. tot expeditionibus, tot proeliis, seu fortitudine adversus hostis seu patientia ac labore paene adversus ipsam rerum naturam opus fuit, neque me militum neque　5 vos ducis paenituit. ergo egressi, ego veterum legatorum, vos priorum exercituum terminos, finem Britanniae non fama nec rumore, sed castris et armis tenemus: inventa Britannia et subacta. equidem saepe in agmine, cum vos paludes montesve et flumina fatigarent, fortissimi cuiusque　10 voces audiebam: 'quando dabitur hostis, quando in manus veniet?' veniunt, e latebris suis extrusi, et vota virtusque in aperto, omniaque prona victoribus atque eadem victis adversa. nam ut superasse tantum itineris, evasisse silvas, transisse aestuaria pulchrum ac decorum in frontem, ita　15 fugientibus periculosissima quae hodie prosperrima sunt; neque enim nobis aut locorum eadem notitia aut commeatuum eadem abundantia, sed manus et arma et in his omnia. quod ad me attinet, iam pridem mihi decretum est neque exercitus neque ducis terga tuta esse. proinde et honesta　20 mors turpi vita potior, et incolumitas ac decus eodem loco sita sunt; nec inglorium fuerit in ipso terrarum ac naturae fine cecidisse.　　　　　　　　　　　　　*ibid.* XXXIII. 2-6

1　Summarise what Agricola says in this section.
2　What is immediately apparent about the attitude of the Roman commander? How far does a change of style emphasise this?
3　How does Agricola court the favour of his men?
4　What is Agricola's attitude to his enemy? How is this brought out?
5　Do you consider this passage carefully composed?
6　Compare the two speeches. Has Tacitus made an effective

contrast between the two leaders? Are both leaders eloquent
after their fashion? What point is Tacitus making by this
contrast (Agricola's speech follows that of Calgacus)?

7 Agricola was Tacitus' father-in-law, and this biography
was written in his honour. What can we infer about the
writer's regard for Agricola in this piece?

62 Blood, toil, tears and sweat

Καὶ οἵδε μὲν προσηκόντως τῇ πόλει τοιοίδε ἐγένοντο· τοὺς
δὲ λοιποὺς χρὴ ἀσφαλεστέραν μὲν εὔχεσθαι, ἀτολμοτέραν
δὲ μηδὲν ἀξιοῦν τὴν ἐς τοὺς πολεμίους διάνοιαν ἔχειν, σκο-
ποῦντας μὴ λόγῳ μόνῳ τὴν ὠφελίαν, ἣν ἄν τις πρὸς οὐδὲν
χεῖρον αὐτοὺς ὑμᾶς εἰδότας μηκύνοι, λέγων ὅσα ἐν τῷ τοὺς   5
πολεμίους ἀμύνεσθαι ἀγαθὰ ἔνεστιν, ἀλλὰ μᾶλλον τὴν τῆς
πόλεως δύναμιν καθ' ἡμέραν ἔργῳ θεωμένους καὶ ἐραστὰς
γιγνομένους αὐτῆς, καὶ ὅταν ὑμῖν μεγάλη δόξῃ εἶναι, ἐν-
θυμουμένους ὅτι τολμῶντες καὶ γιγνώσκοντες τὰ δέοντα
καὶ ἐν τοῖς ἔργοις αἰσχυνόμενοι ἄνδρες αὐτὰ ἐκτήσαντο, καὶ   10
ὁπότε καὶ πείρᾳ του σφαλεῖεν, οὐκ οὖν καὶ τὴν πόλιν γε τῆς
σφετέρας ἀρετῆς ἀξιοῦντες στερίσκειν, κάλλιστον δὲ ἔρανον
αὐτῇ προϊέμενοι. κοινῇ γὰρ τὰ σώματα διδόντες ἰδίᾳ τὸν
ἀγήρων ἔπαινον ἐλάμβανον καὶ τὸν τάφον ἐπισημότατον,
οὐκ ἐν ᾧ κεῖνται μᾶλλον, ἀλλ' ἐν ᾧ ἡ δόξα αὐτῶν παρὰ τῷ   15
ἐντυχόντι αἰεὶ καὶ λόγου καὶ ἔργου καιρῷ αἰείμνηστος κατα-
λείπεται. ἀνδρῶν γὰρ ἐπιφανῶν πᾶσα γῆ τάφος, καὶ οὐ
στηλῶν μόνον ἐν τῇ οἰκείᾳ σημαίνει ἐπιγραφή, ἀλλὰ καὶ ἐν
τῇ μὴ προσηκούσῃ ἄγραφος μνήμη παρ' ἑκάστῳ τῆς γνώ-
μης μᾶλλον ἢ τοῦ ἔργου ἐνδιαιτᾶται. οὓς νῦν ὑμεῖς ζηλώ-   20
σαντες καὶ τὸ εὔδαιμον τὸ ἐλεύθερον, τὸ δ' ἐλεύθερον τὸ
εὔψυχον κρίναντες μὴ περιορᾶσθε τοὺς πολεμικοὺς κινδύ-
νους. οὐ γὰρ οἱ κακοπραγοῦντες δικαιότερον ἀφειδοῖεν ἂν
τοῦ βίου, οἷς ἐλπὶς οὐκ ἔστιν ἀγαθοῦ, ἀλλ' οἷς ἡ ἐναντία
μεταβολὴ ἐν τῷ ζῆν ἔτι κινδυνεύεται καὶ ἐν οἷς μάλιστα   25
μεγάλα τὰ διαφέροντα, ἤν τι πταίσωσιν. ἀλγεινοτέρα γὰρ
ἀνδρί γε φρόνημα ἔχοντι ἡ μετὰ τοῦ ἐν τῷ μαλακισθῆναι
κάκωσις ἢ ὁ μετὰ ῥώμης καὶ κοινῆς ἐλπίδος ἅμα γιγνόμενος
ἀναίσθητος θάνατος.

Thucydides, II. 43 (Funeral Speech)

98

1 To whom does οἵδε in sentence 1 refer?
2 Translate: ἀτολμοτέραν...διάνοιαν ἔχειν (ll. 2–3), ἐν τοῖς
ἔργοις αἰσχυνόμενοι (l. 10), ἀνδρῶν γὰρ ἐπιφανῶν...
ἐνδιαιτᾶται (ll. 17–20).
3 Analyse and comment on the structure of sentence 2
(ll. 11–13).
4 This is supposed to be part of a speech. Does it read like
one? If you find stumbling-blocks to comprehension,
what stylistic features do these contain?
5 Illustrate compression of thought in this passage. Where is
this most effective, where least?
6 Do you find the sentences easily readable, in one breath,
and do they sound fluent? (Consider especially the last
sentence.)
7 Do you find the style of this speech pleasing? Can you
suggest why Thucydides writes likes this? In what is he
particularly successful?

63 Pompey (58) compared with Caesar (52) at the outbreak of civil war

Nec quemquam iam ferre potest Caesarve priorem
Pompeiusve parem. quis iustius induit arma
scire nefas: magno se iudice quisque tuetur;
victrix causa deis placuit sed victa Catoni.
nec coiere pares. alter vergentibus annis   5
in senium longoque togae tranquillior usu
dedidicit iam pace ducem, famaeque petitor
multa dare in volgus, totus popularibus auris
inpelli plausuque sui gaudere theatri,
nec reparare novas vires, multumque priori   10
credere fortunae. stat magni nominis umbra,
qualis frugifero quercus sublimis in agro
exuvias veteris populi sacrataque gestans
dona ducum nec iam validis radicibus haerens
pondere fixa suo est, nudosque per aera ramos   15
effundens trunco, non frondibus, efficit umbram,
et quamvis primo nutet casura sub Euro,
tot circum silvae firmo se robore tollant,

99

sola tamen colitur. sed non in Caesare tantum
nomen erat nec fama ducis, sed nescia virtus   20
stare loco, solusque pudor non vincere bello.
acer et indomitus, quo spes quoque ira vocasset,
ferre manum et numquam temerando parcere ferro,
successus urguere suos, instare favori
numinis, inpellens quidquid sibi summa petenti   25
obstaret gaudensque viam fecisse ruina,
qualiter expressum ventis per nubila fulmen
aetheris inpulsi sonitu mundique fragore
emicuit rupitque diem populosque paventes
terruit obliqua praestringens lumina flamma: 30
in sua templa furit, nullaque exire vetante
materia magnamque cadens magnamque revertens
dat stragem late sparsosque recolligit ignes.

Lucan, Pharsalia I. 125–57

6. *togae*: Pompey was six years older than Caesar.
9. *sui...theatri*: i.e. Pompey had built his own theatre – the first permanent
   theatre at Rome – in the Campus Martius, out of spoils from the Mithri-
   datic War.
31. *templa*: i.e. quarter of the sky.

1 How would you describe the feeling of this description? –
  is it emotional or flat?
2 Examine in detail the two similes (vv. 12–19, 27–33). Are
  they successful? Are they fair in their description of
  Pompey and Caesar?
3 How would you describe the language? Is it economical,
  inflated, objective, restrained, emotional, prosaic, highly
  poetic – or what?
4 Lucan is well known for his ability to sum up persons or
  things in a short epigrammatic phrase. What evidence of
  this ability can you find here?
5 Some scholars would argue that Lucan's style is totally
  unpoetic. Can you see a case for this assertion from this
  passage?
6 'In no poet, except perhaps Ovid or Seneca, is the influence
  of a rhetorical training more striking than in Lucan.' Is
  there evidence of this here?

64 *Dulce et decorum est…?*

Οὓς μὲν γάρ τις ἔπεμψεν
οἶδεν, ἀντὶ δὲ φωτῶν
τεύχη καὶ σποδὸς εἰς ἑκά-
στου δόμους ἀφικνεῖται.

ὁ χρυσαμοιβὸς δ᾽ Ἄρης σωμάτων   5
καὶ ταλαντοῦχος ἐν μάχῃ δορὸς
πυρωθὲν ἐξ Ἰλίου
φίλοισι πέμπει βαρὺ
ψῆγμα δυσδάκρυτον ἀν-
τήνορος σποδοῦ γεμί-   10
ζων λέβητας εὐθέτου.
στένουσι δ᾽ εὖ λέγοντες ἄνδρα τὸν μὲν ὡς μάχης ἴδρις,
τὸν δ᾽ ἐν φοναῖς καλῶς πεσόντ᾽
ἀλλοτρίας διαὶ γυναι-   15
κός. τάδε σῖγά τις βαΰ-
ζει· φθονερὸν δ᾽ ὑπ᾽ ἄλγος ἕρ-
πει προδίκοις Ἀτρείδαις.
οἱ δ᾽ αὐτοῦ περὶ τεῖχος
θήκας Ἰλιάδος γᾶς   20
εὔμορφοι κατέχουσιν· ἐχ-
θρὰ δ᾽ ἔχοντας ἔκρυψεν.

Aeschylus, *Agamemnon* 433–55

1 Treat vv. 1 4 as an introductory statement, and analyse
   the progression of thought of the rest.
2 What is the irony of οἶδεν in v. 2?
3 What imagery is suggested by χρυσαμοιβός, πυρωθέν,
   ψῆγμα, and ταλαντοῦχος? What does γεμίζω (v. 10/11)
   normally mean, and why is it so effective here? Comment
   on the effectiveness of the adjectives applied to ψῆγμα and
   σποδοῦ. Why is εὐθέτου ironical, and how does it continue
   the image begun by χρυσαμοιβός?
4 What major change of direction does the poem take at
   v. 12? If you were an actor, how would you read ἀλλοτρίας
   διαὶ γυναικός (v. 15/16)? How does this change the direction
   yet again?

5 What change in tone occurs at v. 19? What words engender pathos? Comment on the use of κατέχω/ἔχω (vv. 21–2).

6 'It is questionable whether there is anything in Greek Tragedy equal to this passage [i.e. the whole chorus] in beauty and pathos.' From your own reading would you rate this passage so highly?

7 Learn the full stanza by heart.

65 *Varus' disaster revisited*

Germanicus visits the place where Varus (in A.D. 9) had lost three legions to the Germans under Arminius.

Igitur cupido Caesarem invadit solvendi suprema militibus ducique, permoto ad miserationem omni qui aderat exercitu ob propinquos, amicos, denique ob casus bellorum et sortem hominum. praemisso Caecina ut occulta saltuum scrutaretur pontesque et aggeres umido paludum et fallacibus campis 5 inponeret, incedunt maestos locos visuque ac memoria deformis. prima Vari castra lato ambitu et dimensis principiis trium legionum manus ostentabant; dein semiruto vallo, humili fossa accisae iam reliquiae consedisse intellegebantur: medio campi albentia ossa, ut fugerant, ut restiterant, dis- 10 iecta vel aggerata. adiacebant fragmina telorum equorumque artus, simul truncis arborum antefixa ora. lucis propinquis barbarae arae, apud quas tribunos ac primorum ordinum centuriones mactaverant. et cladis eius superstites, pugnam aut vincula elapsi, referebant hic cecidisse legatos, illic raptas 15 aquilas; primum ubi vulnus Varo adactum, ubi infelici dextera et suo ictu mortem invenerit; quo tribunali contionatus Arminius, quot patibula captivis, quae scrobes, utque signis et aquilis per superbiam inluserit.

Igitur Romanus qui aderat exercitus sextum post cladis 20 annum trium legionum ossa, nullo noscente alienas reliquias an suorum humo tegeret, omnis ut coniunctos, ut consanguineos, aucta in hostem ira, maesti simul et infensi condebant. primum extruendo tumulo caespitem Caesar posuit, gratissimo munere in defunctos et praesentibus 25 doloris socius. Tacitus, *Annals* I. 61–2

1 What emotional response is the author seeking to evoke from the reader? How does he seek to do this, and how successful is he?

2 Examine the word-order in sentences 2 and 3 (ll. 4–11). How and for what reasons does it differ from what you might have written?

3 Study sentence 7: *hic...illic...ubi...ubi...quo...quot ...quae...ut* (ll. 14–19). What effect is produced by this rapid scene-changing? Is Tacitus reporting factual detail, or using a pleasing narrative device created by his imagination?

4 What is the force of the long parenthesis in sentence 8: *nullo noscente...aucta in hostes ira* (ll. 21–3)? By the time the eye of the reader arrives at the words *maesti et infesti* is he prepared for them?

5 Where is the author's attitude to Varus' fate most transparent?

6 Illustrate from this passage Tacitus' love of *variation* (especially his avoidance of the obvious words for the sake of variety).

7 What is the general feeling of Tacitus' style? Is it a predominantly balanced, or unbalanced one? How studied is it? Is the effect pleasing or contrived?

66   *A battle description*

Principio ut illo advenimus, ubi primum terram tetigimus,
continuo Amphitruo delegit viros primorum principes;
eos legat, Telobois iubet sententiam ut dicant suam:
si sine vi et sine bello velint rapta et raptores tradere,
si quae asportassent reddere, se exercitum extemplo
     domum   5
redducturum, abituros agró Argivos, pacem atque otium
dare illis; sin aliter sient animati neque dent quae petat,
sese igitur summa vi virisque eorum oppidum
     oppugnassere.
haec ubi Telobois ordiné iterarunt quos praefecerat
Amphitruo, magnanimi viri freti virtute et viribus   10
superbe nimi' ferociter legatos nostros increpant,

respondent bello se et suos tutari posse, proinde uti
propere suis de finibus exercitus deducerent.
haec ubi legati pertulere, Amphitruo castris ilico
producit omnem exercitum. contra Teloboae ex oppido   15
legiones educunt suas nimi' pulchris armis praeditas.
    postquam utrimque exitum est maxuma copia,
    dispertiti viri, dispertiti ordines,
    nostras nos more nostro et modo instruximus
legiones, item hostes contra legiones suas instruont.   20
    deinde utrique imperatores in medium exeunt,
    extra turbam ordinum conloquontur simul.
    convenit, victi utri sint eo proelio,
    urbem, agrum, aras, focos seque uti dederent.
    postquam id actum est, tubae contra utrimque
        occanunt,   25
    consonat terra, clamorem utrimque ecferunt.
    imperator utrimque, hinc et illinc, Iovi
    vota suscipere, utrimque hortari exercitum.
    tum pro se quisque id quod quisq' potest et valet
    edit, ferro ferit, tela frangunt, boat   30
    caelum fremitu virum, ex spiritu atque anhelitu
    nebula constat, cadunt volnerum vi viri.
    denique, ut voluimus, nostra superat manus:
    hostes crebri cadunt, nostri contra ingruont,
    vicimus vi feroces.   35
    sed fugam in se tamen nemo convortitur
    nec recedit loco quin statim rem gerat;
    animam amittunt prius quam loco demigrent:
    quisque ut steterat iacet optinetque ordinem.
    hoc ubi Amphitruo erus conspicatust meus,   40
    ilico equites iubet dextera inducere.
    equites parent citi: ab dextera maxumo
    cum clamore involant impetu alacri,
    foedant et proterunt hostium copias
    iure iniustas.   45

1 Summarise the sense of the narrative, omitting all details of
    poetic description.
2 Is this a vivid battle description? Where does the author
    become most 'poetic'? Where is he most prosaic?

3 Is the language 'epic', archaic, grandiose, stylised, formal – or what? Which of these adjectives describe the passage best, and in what particular places?

4 This passage is often described as 'truly Roman in spirit'. Why? How many specifically Roman references and ideas can you find? (Could this *not* be a translation from a Greek battle scene?)

5 How many *archaic* usages can you find? What might it indicate about the date of composition?

6 How successfully, and by what particular method, does the poet convey the idea of the confusion of battle? How clearly does the *noise* of battle come through?

7 How far does the metre change to represent different phases of the action, and how far is this arbitrary?

8 Taking into account your observations, assign this extract to its author.

PART FOUR

67 The end of Hippolytus

(A)

Αὐτῷ δὲ σὺν κλύδωνι καὶ τρικυμίᾳ
κῦμ' ἐξέθηκε ταῦρον, ἄγριον τέρας·
οὗ πᾶσα μὲν χθὼν φθέγματος πληρουμένη
φρικῶδες ἀντεφθέγγετ', εἰσορῶσι δὲ
κρεῖσσον θέαμα δεργμάτων ἐφαίνετο.   5
εὐθὺς δὲ πώλοις δεινὸς ἐμπίπτει φόβος·
καὶ δεσπότης μὲν ἱππικοῖσιν ἤθεσιν
πολὺς ξυνοικῶν ἥρπασ' ἡνίας χεροῖν,
ἕλκει δὲ κώπην ὥστε ναυβάτης ἀνὴρ
ἱμᾶσιν ἐς τοὔπισθεν ἀρτήσας δέμας·   10
αἱ δ' ἐνδακοῦσαι στόμια πυριγενῆ γναθμοῖς
βίᾳ φέρουσιν, οὔτε ναυκλήρου χερὸς
οὔθ' ἱπποδέσμων οὔτε κολλητῶν ὄχων
μεταστρέφουσαι. κεἰ μὲν ἐς τὰ μαλθακὰ
γαίας ἔχων οἴακας εὐθύνοι δρόμον,   15
προυφαίνετ' ἐς τὸ πρόσθεν, ὥστ' ἀναστρέφειν,
ταῦρος, φόβῳ τέτρωρον ἐκμαίνων ὄχον·
εἰ δ' ἐς πέτρας φέροιντο μαργῶσαι φρένας,
σιγῇ πελάζων ἄντυγι ξυνείπετο
ἐς τοῦθ' ἕως ἔσφηλε κἀνεχαίτισεν,   20
ἁψῖδα πέτρῳ προσβαλὼν ὀχήματος.
σύμφυρτα δ' ἦν ἅπαντα· σύριγγές τ' ἄνω
τροχῶν ἐπήδων ἀξόνων τ' ἐνήλατα.
αὐτὸς δ' ὁ τλήμων ἡνίαισιν ἐμπλακεὶς
δεσμὸν δυσεξήνυστον ἕλκεται δεθείς,   25
σποδούμενος μὲν πρὸς πέτραις φίλον κάρα
θραύων τε σάρκας, δεινὰ δ' ἐξαυδῶν κλύειν·
'στῆτ', ὦ φάτναισι ταῖς ἐμαῖς τεθραμμέναι,
μή μ' ἐξαλείψητ'· ὦ πατρὸς τάλαιν' ἀρά.
τίς ἄνδρ' ἄριστον βούλεται σῶσαι παρών;'   30

Euripides, *Hippolytus* 1213–42

21. ἀψῖδα: outer rim of the wheel.
22. σύριγγες: naves.
23. ἐνήλατα: pins.
26. σποδούμενος: smashing.

(B)

Talis extremo mari
pistrix citatas sorbet aut frangit rates.
tremuere terrae, fugit attonitum pecus
passim per agros nec suos pastor sequi
meminit iuvencos; omnis e saltu fera   5
diffugit, omnis frigido exsanguis metu
venator horret. solus immunis metu
Hippolytus artis continet frenis equos
pavidosque notae vocis hortatu ciet....
inobsequentes protinus frenis equi   10
rapuere currum iamque derrantes via,
quacumque rabidos pavidus evexit furor,
hac ire pergunt seque per scopulos agunt.

At ille, qualis turbido rector mari
ratem retentat, ne det obliquum latus,   15
et arte fluctum fallit, haud aliter citos
currus gubernat. ora nunc pressis trahit
constricta frenis, terga nunc torto frequens
verbere cohercet. sequitur adsiduus comes,
nunc aequa carpens spatia, nunc contra obvius   20
oberrat, omni parte terrorem movens.

Non licuit ultra fugere, nam toto obvius
incurrit ore corniger ponti horridus.
tum vero pavida sonipedes mente exciti
imperia solvunt seque luctantur iugo   25
eripere rectique in pedes iactant onus.
praeceps in ora fusus implicuit cadens
laqueo tenaci corpus et quanto magis
pugnat, sequaces hoc magis nodos ligat.
sensere pecudes facinus – et curru levi,   30
dominante nullo, qua timor iussit ruunt.
talis per auras non suum agnoscens onus
Solique falso creditum indignans diem
Phaethonta currus devio excussit polo.

108

late cruentat arva et inlisum caput   35
scopulis resultat; auferunt dumi comas,
et ora durus pulchra populatur lapis
peritque multo vulnere infelix decor.
moribunda celeres membra provolvunt rotae;
tandemque raptum truncus ambusta sude   40
medium per inguen stipite erecto tenet,
paulumque domino currus affixo stetit.
haesere biiuges vulnere – et pariter moram
dominumque rumpunt. inde semanimem secant
virgulta, acutis asperi vepres rubis   45
omnisque truncus corporis partem tulit.
errant per agros funebris famuli manus,
per illa qua distractus Hippolytus loca
longum cruenta tramitem signat nota,
maestaeque domini membra vestigant canes.   50
      Seneca, *Hippolytus* 1048–108 (with omissions)

2. *pistrix*: sea monster.
19. *comes*: sc. the monster.
26. *recti*: 'rearing up'.
34. *Phaethon*: was the son of Helios, and was killed while attempting to drive
his father's chariot through the heavens

(c)

Cependant sur le dos de la plaine liquide
s'élève à gros bouillons une montagne humide;
l'onde approche, se brise, et vomit à nos yeux,
parmi des flots d'écume, un monstre furieux.
Son front large est armé de cornes menaçantes;   5
tout son corps est couvert d'écailles jaunissantes;
indomptable taureau, dragon impétueux,
sa croupe se recourbe en replis tortueux.
Ses longs mugissements font trembler le rivage...
Hippolyte lui seul, digne fils d'un héros,   10
arrête ses coursiers, saisit ses javelots,
pousse au monstre, et d'un dard lancé d'une main sûre,
il lui fait dans le flanc une large blessure.
De rage et de douleur le monstre bondissant
vient aux pieds des chevaux tomber en mugissant,   15
se roule, et leur présente une gueule enflammée,

qui les couvre de feu, de sang et de fumée.
La frayeur les emporte; et sourds à cette fois,
ils ne connaissent plus ni le frein ni la voix...
A travers les rochers la peur les précipite;   20
L'essieu crie et se rompt. L'intrépide Hippolyte
voit voler en éclats tout son char fracassé;
dans les rênes lui-même il tombe embarassé...
J'ai vu, Seigneur, j'ai vu votre malheureux fils
traîné par les chevaux que sa main a nourris.   25
Il veut les rappeler et sa voix les effraie;
ils courent. Tout son corps n'est bientôt qu'une plaie.

        Racine, *Phèdre* 1513–50

 6. *écailles*: scales.
21. *essieu*: axle.
27. *plaie*: wound.

1 What is the main point of concentration in each of these extracts? What are the salient points in each description? Try to account for the different emphases from what you know about the different authors.

2 How do the descriptions of the monster correspond and differ? In which does his sudden appearance have most impact?

3 How does Hippolytus deal with the bolting of his terrified horses in each account? Are there any significant differences of emphasis?

4 Comment on the images used in each. Which account is rendered most effective? Is there one which might almost be called perfunctory? or overbold? In which are the images most extensively worked out?

5 Which account is the most *dramatic*? Which is the most gruesome and bloodthirsty? (Can you think of any reason for this?) Which extract contains the best poetry? In which are *sound* and *rhythm* most effectively employed?

6 How much *pathos* is there in each account? Say exactly how this is achieved in each case.

7 How much do we learn of the character of Hippolytus in each account? Does it vary much?

8 Examine Racine's narrative and list those ideas, and actual phrases, which he appears to have taken from Euripides on

the one hand and Seneca on the other. Is there any *direct translation* in either the Seneca or the Racine?

68   Sleepless nights — 1

(A)

Jason, in quest of the golden fleece, arrives in Colchis, where King Aeetes (father of Medea) agrees to surrender the fleece only if Jason will perform certain tasks: these include the yoking of two fiery bulls, the sowing of dragon's teeth, and slaying the giants who spring up from the furrows. Medea, in love with Jason, eventually gives him drugs with which to dope the bulls, but not before much heart-searching and hesitation.

Νὺξ μὲν ἔπειτ' ἐπὶ γαῖαν ἄγεν κνέφας, οἱ δ' ἐνὶ πόντῳ
ναυτίλοι εἰς Ἑλίκην τε καὶ ἀστέρας Ὠρίωνος
ἔδρακον ἐκ νηῶν, ὕπνοιο δὲ καί τις ὁδίτης
ἤδη καὶ πυλαωρὸς ἐέλδετο, καί τινα παίδων
μητέρα τεθνεώτων ἀδινὸν περὶ κῶμ' ἐκάλυπτεν,   5
οὐδὲ κυνῶν ὑλακὴ ἔτ' ἀνὰ πτόλιν, οὐ θρόος ἦεν
ἠχήεις, σιγὴ δὲ μελαινυμένην ἔχεν ὄρφνην·
ἀλλὰ μάλ' οὐ Μήδειαν ἐπὶ γλυκερὸς λάβεν ὕπνος.
πολλὰ γὰρ Αἰσονίδαο πόθῳ μελεδήματ' ἔγειρεν
δειδυῖαν ταύρων κρατερὸν μένος, οἷσιν ἔμελλεν   10
φθεῖσθαι ἀεικελίῃ μοίρῃ κατὰ νειὸν Ἄρηος.
δάκρυ δ' ἀπ' ὀφθαλμῶν ἐλέῳ ῥέεν· ἔνδοθι δ' αἰεὶ
τεῖρ' ὀδύνη, σμύχουσα διὰ χροὸς ἀμφί τ' ἀραιὰς
ἶνας καὶ κεφαλῆς ὑπὸ νείατον ἰνίον ἄχρις,
ἔνθ' ἀλεγεινότατον δύνει ἄχος, ὁππότ' ἀνίας   15
ἀκάματοι πραπίδεσσιν ἐνισκίμψωσιν ἔρωτες.
πυκνὰ δέ οἱ κραδίη στηθέων ἔντοσθεν ἔθυιεν,
ἠελίου ὥς τίς τε δόμοις ἔνι πάλλεται αἴγλη,
ὕδατος ἐξανιοῦσα τὸ δὴ νέον ἠὲ λέβητι
ἠέ που ἐν γαυλῷ κέχυται, ἡ δ' ἔνθα καὶ ἔνθα   20
ὠκείῃ στροφάλιγγι τινάσσεται ἀίσσουσα —
ὣς δὲ καὶ ἐν στήθεσσι κέαρ ἐλελίζετο κούρης,
φῆ δέ οἱ ἄλλοτε μὲν θελκτήρια φάρμακα ταύρων
δωσέμεν· ἄλλοτε δ' οὔτι, καταφθεῖσθαι δὲ καὶ αὐτή·

αὐτίκα δ' οὔτ' αὐτὴ θανέειν, οὐ φάρμακα δώσειν, 25
ἀλλ' αὔτως εὔκηλος ἐὴν ὀτλησέμεν ἄτην.
ἐ3ομένη δῆπειτα δοάσσατο, φώνησέν τε·
'Δειλὴ ἐγώ, νῦν ἔνθα κακῶν ἢ ἔνθα γένωμαι;
πάντη μοι φρένες εἰσὶν ἀμήχανοι, οὐδέ τις ἀλκὴ
πήματος, ἀλλ' αὔτως φλέγει ἔμπεδον. ὡς ὄφελόν γε 30
'Αρτέμιδος κραιπνοῖσι πάρος βελέεσσι δαμῆναι,
πρὶν τόνγ' εἰσιδέειν, πρὶν 'Αχαιίδα νῆα κομίσσαι.'
Apollonius Rhodius, *Argonautica* III. 744–75

2. Ἑλίκην... Ὠρίωνος: the Bear, and the stars of Orion.
4. πυλαωρός: warder.
10. ταύρων: see introductory note.
13. σμύχουσα: smouldering.
16. ἐνισκίμψωσιν: aim.
17. ἔθυϊεν: throbbed.
20. γαυλῷ: pail.
24. δωσέμεν: δώσειν (cf. v. 25).
26. ὀτλησέμεν: to endure.
27. δοάσσατο: 'she wavered in mind'.
31. 'Αρτέμιδος: Artemis, goddess of archery.

(B)

Dido, knowing that Aeneas is leaving her, passes a night in
bitterness and misery:

Nox erat et placidum carpebant fessa soporem
corpora per terras, silvaeque et saeva quierant
aequora, cum medio volvuntur sidera lapsu,
cum tacet omnis ager, pecudes pictaeque volucres,
quaeque lacus late liquidos quaeque aspera dumis 5
rura tenent, somno positae sub nocte silenti.
at non infelix animi Phoenissa, neque umquam
solvitur in somnos oculisve aut pectore noctem
accipit: ingeminant curae rursusque resurgens
saevit amor magnoque irarum fluctuat aestu. 10
sic adeo insistit secumque ita corde volutat:
'en, quid ago? rursusne procos inrisa priores
experiar, Nomadumque petam conubia supplex,
quos ego sim totiens iam dedignata maritos?
Iliacas igitur classis atque ultima Teucrum 15

iussa sequar? quiane auxilio iuvat ante levatos
et bene apud memores veteris stat gratia facti?
quis me autem, fac velle, sinet ratibusve superbis
invisam accipiet? nescis heu, perdita, necdum
Laomedonteae sentis periuria gentis?   20
quid tum? sola fuga nautas comitabor ovantis?
an Tyriis omnique manu stipata meorum
inferar et, quos Sidonia vix urbe revelli,
rursus agam pelago et ventis dare vela iubebo?
quin morere ut merita es, ferroque averte dolorem.   25
tu lacrimis evicta meis, tu prima furentem
his, germana, malis oneras atque obicis hosti.
non licuit thalami expertem sine crimine vitam
degere more ferae, talis nec tangere curas;
non servata fides cineri promissa Sychaeo.'   30
                                   Virgil, *Aeneid* IV. 522–52

7. *Phoenissa*: i.e. Dido.
13. *Nomadum*: African tribes living around Carthage.
18. *fac velle*: 'supposing that I wished to'.
20. *Laomedonteae*: i.e. Trojan. Laomedon was a king of Troy.

1 Medea and Dido are both having sleepless nights in an
   agony of indecision. Do the passages reveal similarity of
   treatment, or not? Which poet places more emphasis on
   the idea of sleeplessness, and which on indecision?
2 Is the attitude of the two poets at all similar?
3 Both poets spend some time describing the night scene outside before returning to the heroine; why? How far are
   they successful in the effect they are trying to achieve?
4 Do you find Dido or Medea more pitiable in these extracts?
   Why?
5 Do you see any echoes of Apollonius' description in the
   description of Virgil?
6 Is Apollonius' simile (vv. 18–21) apt?
7 Do the feelings of the two heroines differ? Is the emotional atmosphere similar, or not?
8 Do you consider the style of (A) to be Homeric? If so, say
   in what way. If not, say how it differs.
9 'We find quite artful onomatopoeia in Apollonius, but not
   the emotive effects of Virgil. As compared with Virgil,

Apollonius is still Homeric – i.e. he still retains the Homeric objectivity' (Brooks Otis, *Virgil* 89 n., and see 85–6.). Discuss.

69 *Sleepless nights — 2*

(c) The poet settles down to sleep one night, but is assailed by Love, and rebuked for his slackness in the god's service:

> Lecto compositus vix prima silentia noctis
> > carpebam et somno lumina victa dabam,
> cum me saevus Amor prensat sursumque capillis
> > excitat et lacerum pervigilare iubet.
> 'tu famulus meus,' inquit, 'ames cum mille puellas,   5
> > solus, io, solus, dure, iacere potes?'
> exsilio et pedibus nudis tunicaque soluta
> > omne iter impedio, nullum iter expedio.
> nunc propero, nunc ire piget, rursumque redire
> > paenitet, et pudor est stare via media.   10
> ecce tacent voces hominum strepitusque viarum
> > et volucrum cantus turbaque fida canum:
> solus ego ex cunctis paveo somnumque torumque,
> > et sequor imperium, magne Cupido, tuum.
> > > > Petronius, fragment 38 (Ernout)

4. *lacerum*: tr. 'in torment'.
6. *io*: ho, there!
8. *expedio*: complete.

1 What is the reason for Petronius' abortive expedition?
2 Is the mood of these lines serious, or witty and sophisticated, or what? Do they make a point?
3 How successful is the description of the deserted night-scene?
4 Petronius' lyrics have been much admired. Would you call this first-rate elegiac poetry? Is the versification skilful?
5 Do you think that this fragment is likely to be a complete poem?

(D) The following is a well known 'sonnet' from the *Silvae* of Statius:

SOMNUS

Crimine quo merui iuvenis, placidissime divum,
quove errore miser, donis ut solus egerem,
Somne, tuis? tacet omne pecus volucresque feraeque
et simulant fessos curvata cacumina somnos,
nec trucibus fluviis idem sonus; occidit horror   5
aequoris, et terris fluaria acclinata quiescunt.
septima iam rediens Phoebe mihi respicit aegras
stare genas; totidem Oetaeae Paphiaeque recursant
lampades et totiens nostros Tithonia questus
praeterit et gelido spargit miserata flagello   10
unde ego sufficiam? non si mihi lumina mille
quae sacer alterna tantum statione tenebat
Argus et haud umquam vigilabat corpore toto.
at nunc heu! si aliquis longa sub nocte puellae
brachia nexa tenens ultro te, Somne, repellit: 15
inde veni! nec te totas infundere pennas
luminibus compello meis (hoc turba precetur
laetior): extremo me tange cacumine virgae
(sufficit) aut leviter suspenso poplite transi.

Statius, Silvae v. 4

7. *Phoebe*: a name given to the moon.
8. *Oetaeae Paphiaeque*: the evening and morning star
9. *Tithonia*: the dawn; the *flagellum* is the whip with which she chases the stars away.
13. *Argus*: Juno set this herdsman, who had eyes all over his body, to watch over Io.

1 Does the poem strike you as serious, or more of an 'occasional piece'? Give reasons for your answer.

2 Summarise the sense of the poem. It falls into several stages – what are they? Is the progression logical and satisfying?

3 How would you describe the tone of vv. 11–13 (*non si mihi...toto*)? Witty, humorous, tongue-in-cheek, or quite serious?

4 *si aliquis...luminibus compello meis* (vv. 14–17). Does this strike you as artificial, witty, ingenious – or what? Is it i

keeping with the spirit of the rest of the poem, or out of place?

5 Attempt a translation of the whole poem, aiming to get as near the spirit of the original as possible.

6 What was the *intention* of the poet in writing such a poem? Is it successful? If in your opinion it fails, state why.

(E)

How many thousand of my poorest subjects
are at this hour asleep! O sleep! O gentle sleep!
Nature's soft nurse, how have I frighted thee,
that thou no more will weigh my eyelids down
and steep my senses in forgetfulness?   5
Why rather, sleep, liest thou in smoky cribs,
upon uneasy pallets stretching thee,
and hush'd with buzzing night-flies to thy slumber,
than in the perfumed chambers of the great,
under the canopies of costly state,   10
and lull'd with sounds of sweetest melody?
O, thou dull god! why liest thou with the vile,
in loathsome beds, and leavest the kingly couch,
a watch-case, or a common larum-bell?
Wilt thou upon the high and giddy mast   15
seal up the ship-boy's eyes, and rock his brains
in cradle of the rude imperious surge,
and in the visitation of the winds,
who take the ruffian billows by the top,
curling their monstrous heads, and hanging them   20
with deafening clamours in the slippery clouds,
that, with the hurly, death itself awakes?
Canst thou, O partial sleep! give thy repose
to the wet sea-boy in an hour so rude;
and in the calmest and most stillest night,   25
with all appliances and means to boot
deny it to a king? Then, happy low, lie down!
Uneasy lies the head that wears a crown.

Shakespeare, *Henry IV Part 2*, Act III, i

116

1 What similarities are there between this speech and the poem of Statius?

2 What theme runs through all three of these pieces concerned with sleepless nights, and in which is it most vividly described?

3 Are the two Latin poems similar in intention?

4 What are the essential differences between the personification of Sleep in (D) and (E)?

70 The big fight — 1

'As Cooper moved away the blood was spurting from his eyebrow. As so often before, the scars of many battles had betrayed him and although it was several seconds before the referee stepped in, the end was already inevitable.   5

In those seconds, plunging forward like a wounded bull, Cooper strove gallantly to snatch victory against impossible odds. But the blood was blinding him. Clay, unmarked, danced out of range and around the ring cries of "stop 10 it!" drowned the cheers.'

Sunday Telegraph, 22 May 1966

List the poetical language – the images, and figures of speech – used in this extract. Would you call this an exciting narrative – good journalism – or not? Give reasons.

(A)

Now read Homer's account of a boxing match between Epeius and Euryalus.

Εὐρύαλος δέ οἱ οἶος ἀνίστατο, ἰσόθεος φώς,
Μηκιστῆος υἱὸς Ταλαϊονίδαο ἄνακτος,
ὅς ποτε Θήβασδ' ἤλθε δεδουπότος Οἰδιπόδαο
ἐς τάφον· ἔνθα δὲ πάντας ἐνίκα Καδμείωνας.
τὸν μὲν Τυδεΐδης δουρικλυτὸς ἀμφεπονεῖτο   5
θαρσύνων ἔπεσιν, μέγα δ' αὐτῷ βούλετο νίκην.
ζῶμα δέ οἱ πρῶτον παρακάββαλεν, αὐτὰρ ἔπειτα
δῶκεν ἱμάντας ἐυτμήτους βοὸς ἀγραύλοιο.
τὼ δὲ ζωσαμένω βήτην ἐς μέσσον ἀγῶνα,

ἄντα δ' ἀνασχομένω χερσὶ στιβαρῇσιν ἅμ' ἄμφω   10
σύν ῥ' ἔπεσον, σὺν δέ σφι βαρεῖαι χεῖρες ἔμιχθεν
δεινὸς δὲ χρόμαδος γενύων γένετ', ἔρρεε δ' ἱδρὼς
πάντοθεν ἐκ μελέων· ἐπὶ δ' ὤρνυτο δῖος Ἐπειός,
κόψε δὲ παπτήναντα παρήιον· οὐδ' ἄρ' ἔτι δὴν
ἑστήκειν· αὐτοῦ γὰρ ὑπήριπε φαίδιμα γυῖα.   15
ὡς δ' ὅθ' ὑπὸ φρικὸς Βορέω ἀναπάλλεται ἰχθὺς
θίν' ἐν φυκιόεντι, μέλαν δέ ἑ κῦμα κάλυψεν,
ὣς πληγεὶς ἀνέπαλτο. ἀτὰρ μεγάθυμος Ἐπειὸς
χερσὶ λαβὼν ὤρθωσε· φίλοι δ' ἀμφέσταν ἑταῖροι,
οἵ μιν ἄγον δι' ἀγῶνος ἐφελκομένοισι πόδεσσιν   20
αἷμα παχὺ πτύοντα, κάρη βάλλονθ' ἑτέρωσε·
κὰδ δ' ἀλλοφρονέοντα μετὰ σφίσιν εἶσαν ἄγοντες,
αὐτοὶ δ' οἰχόμενοι κόμισαν δέπας ἀμφικύπελλον...

Homer, *Iliad* XXIII. 677–99

3. δεδουπότος: fallen (in death).
7. ζῶμα: loin-cloth.
8. ἱμάντας: leather thongs wound round the knuckles.
12. χρόμαδος: grinding.
15. αὐτοῦ: on the spot.
17. φυκιόεντι: covered with sea-weed.

(B)

Compare the fight between Entellus and Dares as described
by Virgil:

Haec fatus duplicem ex umeris reiecit amictum
et magnos membrorum artus, magna ossa lacertosque
exuit atque ingens media consistit harena.
tum satus Anchisa caestus pater extulit aequos
et paribus palmas amborum innexuit armis.   5
constitit in digitos extemplo arrectus uterque
bracchiaque ad superas interritus extulit auras.
abduxere retro longe capita ardua ab ictu
immiscentque manus manibus pugnamque lacessunt,
ille pedum melior motu fretusque iuventa,   10
hic membris et mole valens; sed tarda trementi
genua labant, vastos quatit aeger anhelitus artus.

multa viri nequiquam inter se vulnera iactant,
multa cavo lateri ingeminant et pectore vastos
dant sonitus, erratque auris et tempora circum 15
crebra manus, duro crepitant sub vulnere malae.
stat gravis Entellus nisuque immotus eodem
corpore tela modo atque oculis vigilantibus exit.
ille, velut celsam oppugnat qui molibus urbem
aut montana sedet circum castella sub armis, 20
nunc hos, nunc illos aditus, omnemque pererrat
arte locum et variis adsultibus inritus urget.
ostendit dextram insurgens Entellus et alte
extulit, ille ictum venientem a vertice velox
praevidit celerique elapsus corpore cessit; 25
Entellus viris in ventum effudit et ultro
ipse gravis graviterque ad terram pondere vasto
concidit, ut quondam cava concidit aut Erymantho
aut Ida in magna radicibus eruta pinus.
consurgunt studiis Teucri et Trinacria pubes; 30
it clamor caelo primusque accurrit Acestes
aequaevumque ab humo miserans attollit amicum.
at non tardatus casu neque territus heros
acrior ad pugnam redit ac vim suscitat ira;
tum pudor incendit viris et conscia virtus, 35
praecipitemque Daren ardens agit aequore toto
nunc dextra ingeminans ictus, nunc ille sinistra.
nec mora nec requies: quam multa grandine nimbi
culminibus crepitant, sic densis ictibus heros
creber utraque manu pulsat versatque Dareta. 40

Virgil, *Aeneid* v. 421–60

4. *caestus*: boxing gloves which contained metal.
28–9. *Erymanthus* and *Ida* were famous mountains in Arcadia and Troy.

1 Virgil plainly had Homer's boxing match in mind when he
  wrote this famous passage: list all the similarities you can
  detect.
2 Why does Epeius win his contest? Why does Entellus win
  his? What kind of a clue might this give us to the *intention*
  of the different poets?
3 What are the essential differences between the two accounts? Which is the more effective? Why?

4 Virgil's account has been called 'psychological drama'; do you agree? If this is a drama, how would you describe Homer's account?

5 Do we sympathise with the winner in each case, or the loser, or neither? What is there in the language which makes us feel this way?

6 Note the similes in each piece (three of Virgil's to one of Homer's); which are most effective? Why does Virgil use them at all in the middle of an exciting piece of narrative? Explain the Homeric simile in detail. What do you think a successful simile must do?

7 What are the emotions described in Virgil's piece to cause the come-back of the aging Entellus and his subsequent victory? Does this help in our consideration of the match as 'psychological drama'?

8 Explain how Virgil produces the effect of confused, hand-to-hand fighting in vv. 9–16.

9 Put the whole of the Latin piece into modern English, such as you might read in a newspaper the morning after the big fight (see above). Now try the same with the Homeric account. Which is harder, and why?

71   *The big fight — 2*

Compare the following two accounts of the same fight:

(c) AMYCUS V. POLYDEUCES

Οἱ δ' ἐπεὶ οὖν ἐν ἱμᾶσι διασταδὸν ἠρτύναντο,
αὐτίκ' ἀνασχόμενοι ῥεθέων προπάροιθε βαρείας
χεῖρας, ἐπ' ἀλλήλοισι μένος φέρον ἀντιόωντες.
ἔνθα δὲ Βεβρύκων μὲν ἄναξ, ἅτε κῦμα θαλάσσης
τρηχὺ θοῇ ἐπὶ νηὶ κορύσσεται, ἡ δ' ὑπὸ τυτθὸν   5
ἱδρείῃ πυκινοῖο κυβερνητῆρος ἀλύσκει
ἱεμένου φορέεσθαι ἔσω τοίχοιο κλύδωνος —
ὣς ὅγε Τυνδαρίδην φοβέων ἕπετ' οὐδέ μιν εἴα
δηθύνειν, ὁ δ' ἄρ' αἰὲν ἀνούτατος ἦν διὰ μῆτιν
ἀίσσοντ' ἀλέεινεν. ἀπηνέα δ' αἶψα νοήσας   10
πυγμαχίην, ᾗ κάρτος ἀάατος ᾗ τε χερείων,

120

στῆ ῥ' ἄμοτον καὶ χερσὶν ἐναντία χεῖρας ἔμειξεν.
ὡς δ' ὅτε νήια δοῦρα θοοῖς ἀντίξοα γόμφοις
ἀνέρες ὑληουργοὶ ἐπιβλήδην ἐλάοντες
θείνωσι σφύρῃσιν, ἐπ' ἄλλῳ δ' ἄλλος ἄηται   15
δοῦπος ἄδην — ὣς τοῖσι παρήιά τ' ἀμφοτέρωθεν
καὶ γένυες κτύπεον, βρυχὴ δ' ὑπετέλλετ' ὀδόντων
ἄσπετος· οὐδ' ἔλληξαν ἐπισταδὸν οὐτάζοντες
ἔστε περ οὐλοὸν ἄσθμα καὶ ἀμφοτέρους ἐδάμασσεν.
στάντε δὲ βαιὸν ἄπωθεν ἀπωμόρξαντο μετώπων   20
ἱδρῶ ἅλις, καματηρὸν ἀυτμένα φυσιόωντε.
ἂψ δ' αὖτις συνόρουσαν ἐναντίω, ἠύτε ταύρω
φορβάδος ἀμφὶ βοὸς κεκοτηότε δηριάασθον.
ἔνθα δ' ἔπειτ' Ἄμυκος μὲν ἐπ' ἀκροτάτοισιν ἀερθεὶς
βουτύπος οἷα πόδεσσι τανύσσατο, κὰδ δὲ βαρεῖαν   25
χεῖρ' ἐπὶ οἷ πελέμιξεν· ὁ δ' ἀίσσοντος ὑπέστη,
κρᾶτα παρακλίνας, ὤμῳ δ' ἀνεδέξατο πῆχυν.
τυτθὸν δ' ἄνδιχα τοῖο παρὲκ γόνυ γουνὸς ἀμείβων,
κόψε μεταΐγδην ὑπὲρ οὔατος, ὀστέα δ' εἴσω
ῥῆξεν· ὁ δ' ἀμφ' ὀδύνῃ γνὺξ ἤριπεν. οἱ δ' ἰάχησαν   30
ἥρωες Μινύαι· τοῦ δ' ἀθρόος ἔκχυτο θυμός.

Apollonius Rhodius, *Argonautica* II. 67–97

4. The *Bebryces* were natives of the land where the Argonauts have put in.
8. *Tyndarides* = Polydeuces (Latin *Pollux*).
14. ὑληουργοί: shipwrights.
24. *Amycus*: king of the Bebryces.
31. Μινύαι: originally a race of heroes in Orchomenus, but the name is also used of the Argonauts.

1 Would you have thought the author to be Homer, if the name of Apollonius Rhodius had not been supplied? If not, give reasons.

2 How far does this account reflect the language of Homer's boxing match, and how much of Apollonius Rhodius can we see in the Virgil passage?

3 (a) Criticise in detail the application of the two similes at vv. 4–8 and 13–16.
(b) Does the sudden change of type of simile (from ships to animals) necessarily upset the general flow of things?

4 How does this account compare with those of Homer and Virgil in descriptive power? Why does Polydeuces win?

5 What contrasts does Apollonius Rhodius make between

the contestants? Are they the same contrasts as those which
Virgil makes? (Cf. Theocritus' account below.)

6 Do you think Apollonius Rhodius' indecisive first round
is dramatically effective? Compare the course of his fight
with the others.

(D)

Compare with this an account of the same fight by Theocritus:

Οἳ δ' ἐπεὶ οὖν σπείρῃσιν ἐκαρτύναντο βοείαις
χεῖρας καὶ περὶ γυῖα μακροὺς εἵλιξαν ἱμάντας,
ἐς μέσσον σύναγον φόνον ἀλλήλοισι πνέοντες.
ἔνθα πολύς σφισι μόχθος ἐπειγομένοισιν ἐτύχθη
ὁππότερος κατὰ νῶτα λάβοι φάος ἠελίοιο.   5
ἰδρείῃ μέγαν ἄνδρα παρήλυθες, ὦ Πολύδευκες,
βάλλετο δ' ἀκτίνεσσιν ἅπαν Ἀμύκοιο πρόσωπον.
αὐτὰρ ὅγ' ἐν θυμῷ κεχολωμένος ἵετο πρόσσω,
χερσὶ τιτυσκόμενος. τοῦ δ' ἄκρον τύψε γένειον
Τυνδαρίδης ἐπιόντος· ὀρίνθη δὲ πλέον ἢ πρίν,   10
σὺν δὲ μάχην ἐτάραξε, πολὺς δ' ἐπέκειτο νενευκὼς
ἐς γαῖαν. Βέβρυκες δ' ἐπαΰτεον, οἱ δ' ἑτέρωθεν
ἥρωες κρατερὸν Πολυδεύκεα θαρσύνεσκον,
δειδιότες μή πώς μιν ἐπιβρίσας δαμάσειε
χώρῳ ἐνὶ στεινῷ Τιτυῷ ἐναλίγκιος ἀνήρ.   15
ἤτοι ὅγ' ἔνθα καὶ ἔνθα παριστάμενος Διὸς υἱὸς
ἀμφοτέρῃσιν ἄμυσσεν ἀμοιβαδίς, ἔσχεθε δ' ὁρμῆς
παῖδα Ποσειδάωνος ὑπερφίαλόν περ ἐόντα.
ἔστη δὲ πληγαῖς μεθύων, ἐκ δ' ἔπτυσεν αἷμα
φοίνιον· οἱ δ' ἅμα πάντες ἀριστῆες κελάδησαν,   20
ὡς ἴδον ἕλκεα λυγρὰ περὶ στόμα τε γναθμούς τε·
ὄμματα δ' οἰδήσαντος ἀπεστείνωτο προσώπου.
τὸν μὲν ἄναξ ἐτάρασσεν ἐτώσια χερσὶ προδεικνὺς
πάντοθεν· ἀλλ' ὅτε δή μιν ἀμηχανέοντ' ἐνόησε,
μέσσης ῥινὸς ὕπερθε κατ' ὀφρύος ἤλασε πυγμῇ,   25
πᾶν δ' ἀπέσυρε μέτωπον ἐς ὀστέον. αὐτὰρ ὃ πληγεὶς
ὕπτιος ἐν φύλλοισι τεθηλόσιν ἐξετανύσθη.
ἔνθα μάχη δριμεῖα πάλιν γένετ' ὀρθωθέντος,
ἀλλήλους δ' ὄλεκον στερεοῖς θείνοντες ἱμᾶσιν.
ἀλλ' ὁ μὲν ἐς στῆθός τε καὶ ἔξω χεῖρας ἐνώμα   30
αὐχένος ἀρχηγὸς Βεβρύκων· ὁ δ' ἀεικέσι πληγαῖς

πᾶν συνέφυρε πρόσωπον ἀνίκητος Πολυδεύκης.
σάρκες δ' ᾧ μὲν ἱδρῶτι συνίζανον, ἐκ μεγάλου δὲ
αἶψ' ὀλίγος γένετ' ἀνδρός· ὃ δ' αἰεὶ πάσσονα γυῖα
αὐξομένου φορέεσκε πόνου καὶ χροιῇ ἀμείνω.   35
  Ἤτοι ὅγε ῥέξαι τι λιλαιόμενος μέγα ἔργον
σκαιῇ μὲν σκαιὴν Πολυδεύκεος ἔλλαβε χεῖρα,
δοχμὸς ἀπὸ προβολῆς κλινθείς, ἑτέρῳ δ' ἐπιβαίνων
δεξιτερῆς ἤνεγκεν ἀπὸ λαγόνος πλατὺ γυῖον.
καί κε τυχὼν ἔβλαψεν Ἀμυκλαίων βασιλῆα,   40
ἀλλ' ὅγ' ὑπεξανέδυ κεφαλῇ στιβαρῇ ἅμα χειρὶ
πλῆξεν ὑπὸ σκαιὸν κρόταφον καὶ ἐπέμπεσεν ὤμῳ·
ἐκ δ' ἐχύθη μέλαν αἷμα θοῶς κροτάφοιο χανόντος·
λαιῇ δὲ στόμα κόψε, πυκνοὶ δ' ἀράβησαν ὀδόντες·
αἰεὶ δ' ὀξυτέρῳ πιτύλῳ δηλεῖτο πρόσωπον   45
μέχρι συνηλοίησε παρήια. πᾶς δ' ἐπὶ γαίῃ
κεῖτ' ἀλλοφρονέων καὶ ἀνέσχεθε νεῖκος ἀπαυδῶν
ἀμφοτέρας ἅμα χεῖρας, ἐπεὶ θανάτου σχεδὸν ἦεν.
τὸν μὲν ἄρα κρατέων περ ἀτάσθαλον οὐδὲν ἔρεξας,
ὦ πύκτη Πολύδευκες· ὄμοσσε δέ τοι μέγαν ὅρκον, 50
ὃν πατέρ' ἐκ πόντοιο Ποσειδάωνα κικλήσκων,
μήποτ' ἔτι ξείνοισιν ἑκὼν ἀνιηρὸς ἔσεσθαι.

Theocritus, *Idyll* XXII. 80–134 (om. 115–17)

15. Τιτυῷ: Tityos was a mythical giant.
17. ἄμυσσεν: cut.
18. Ποσειδάωνος = Amycus.
23. ἐτώσια κ.τ.λ.: i.e. blows threatened, but not delivered.
33. συνίζανον: collapsed, fell in.
40. Ἀμυκλαίων β.: i.e. Polydeuces.
51. ὅν: i.e. Amycus'.

1 What is the point of νενευκώς in v. 11? What does it tell us?
2 What does ἔξω... αὐχένος (v. 30–1) mean? Why are these
   blows referred to as ἀεικέσι πληγαῖς?
3 Translate vv. 34–5; what exactly does this mean?
4 Note all the verbal echoes you can find from Homer and
   Apollonius Rhodius. On which account does Theocritus
   seem to rely more heavily?
5 How does this passage differ from those of Homer and
   Apollonius Rhodius? Is the style generally similar, or not?
   Does this account differ in any *detail* from the others?
6 Find the Greek for the following boxing terms: 'feint';

'point' of the chin; 'punch-drunk' (groggy); dazed; spit blood; 'laid out'; 'throw in the towel'; 'flicking out rights and lefts'.

7 Can you account for the all but total exclusion of simile from this passage?

8 Does the *tone* of this passage differ in any way from that of the others?

9 Which of all these four pieces is (*a*) most realistic, (*b*) most dramatic, and (*c*) most poetic?

72 *Intimations of immortality*

(A)

Exegi monumentum aere perennius
regalique situ pyramidum altius,
quod non imber edax, non Aquilo impotens
possit diruere aut innumerabilis
annorum series et fuga temporum.   5
non omnis moriar, multaque pars mei
vitabit Libitinam: usque ego postera
crescam laude recens, dum Capitolium
scandet cum tacita virgine pontifex.
dicar, qua violens obstrepit Aufidus   10
et qua pauper aquae Daunus agrestium
regnavit populorum, ex humili potens
princeps Aeolium carmen ad Italos
deduxisse modos. sume superbiam
quaesitam meritis et mihi Delphica   15
lauro cinge volens, Melpomene, comam.

Horace, *Odes* III. 30

(Compare especially (B. iii) below.)

1 Was Horace merely being conceited, or can he be excused in some way?

2 Explain the meaning of vv. 13–14.

3 Can you detect any Grecisms? What are they? Why do you think Horace used them here?

4 Is Horace's claim justified? If not, to whom does the honour

properly belong? (Or have we misunderstood his claim?) What claim might he have made?

(B)

Here are three examples of *Ovid's* literary boasting: (ii) is his epilogue to the *Metamorphoses*.

(i) Quid mihi, Livor edax, ignavos obicis annos
      ingeniique vocas carmen inertis opus,
  non me more patrum, dum strenua sustinet aetas,
      praemia militiae pulverulenta sequi
  nec me verbosas leges ediscere nec me   5
      ingrato vocem prostituisse foro?
  mortale est, quod quaeris, opus; mihi fama perennis
      quaeritur, in toto semper ut orbe canar...
  pascitur in vivis Livor; post fata quiescit,
      cum suus ex merito quemque tuetur honos: 10
  ergo etiam cum me supremus adederit ignis,
      vivam, parsque mei multa superstes erit.
Ovid, Amores I. 15. 1–8, 39–42

(ii) Iamque opus exegi, quod nec Iovis ira nec ignis
  nec poterit ferrum nec edax abolere vetustas.
  cum volet, illa dies, quae nil nisi corporis huius
  ius habet, incerti spatium mihi finiat aevi:
  parte tamen meliore mei super alta perennis   5
  astra ferar, nomenque erit indelebile nostrum,
  quaque patet domitis Romana potentia terris,
  ore legar populi, perque omnia saecula fama,
  siquid habent veri vatum praesagia, vivam!
Ovid, Metamorphoses XV. 871–9

(iii)   Mantua Vergilio gaudet, Verona Catullo;
     Paelignae dicar gloria gentis ego.
Ovid, Amores III. 15. 7–8

1 In each of these pieces there are distinct echoes of Horace's words. Make a detailed list of these similarities. Which piece is closest in spirit to what Horace says?

2 Compare the lists of destructive forces which both poets say their work will survive. Comment on the imagery employed. Which is more effective in painting the picture of Time the Destroyer?

3 How does Ovid use *paradox* to emphasise the idea of 'eternity'?

4 The first piece (B. i) is angled rather differently. Summarise the sense and state exactly how it differs in approach from the more usual boast (A and B. ii).

5 Did Ovid achieve his boast, or more than he boasted – or not? On what would you say his fame chiefly rests today?

(c) Propertius claims to be the first 'Hellenistic' poet of Rome:

> Callimachi Manes et Coi sacra Philitae,
>   in vestrum, quaeso, me sinite ire nemus.
> primus ego ingredior puro de fonte sacerdos
>   Itala per Graios orgia ferre choros.
> dicite, quo pariter carmen tenuastis in antro?   5
>   quove pede ingressi? quamve bibistis aquam?
> a valeat, Phoebum quicumque moratur in armis!
>   exactus tenui pumice versus eat, –
> quo me Fama levat terra sublimis, et a me
>   nata coronatis Musa triumphat equis,   10
> et mecum in curru parvi vectantur Amores,
>   scriptorumque meas turba secuta rotas.

Propertius III. 1. 1–12

(Cf. also III. 2 which is on the same theme.)

1 Look up Callimachus and Philitas (also spelt Philetas) of Cos. Who are they, what did they write, and why does Propertius appeal to them in particular?

2 Propertius, like Horace, claims to have been the first to achieve something in the field of poetry. What was it? Explain the language used in this 'boast' and compare it with that of Horace. Was Propertius' claim justified or not?

3 How does this 'boast' differ from the others, if at all?

The Immortal Bard:

> Not marble, nor the gilded monuments
> of princes, shall outlive this powerful rhyme;
> but you shall shine more bright in these contents
> than unswept stone, besmear'd with sluttish time.
> When wasteful war shall statues overturn,   5
> and broils root out the work of masonry,
> nor Mars his sword nor war's quick fire shall burn
> the living record of your memory.
>
> Shakespeare, *Sonnet* 55. 1–8

1   Compare Shakespeare's list of destructive forces with those
    of Horace, Ovid and Propertius. Do you think Shake-
    speare had the Latin poets in mind when he made this
    'boast'?

2   There is a slight 'twist' revealed in vv. 3 and 8, which sets
    this boast apart from the others. What is it? Compare
    Propertius III. 2. 17–26:

> Fortunata, meo si qua es celebrata libello!
>   carmina erunt formae tot monumenta tuae.
> nam neque Pyramidum sumptus ad sidera ducti,
>   nec Iovis Elei caelum imitata domus,
> nec Mausolei dives fortuna sepulcri   5
>   mortis ab extrema condicione vacant.
> aut illis flamma aut imber subducet honores,
>   annorum aut ictu, pondere victa, ruent.
> at non ingenio quaesitum nomen ab aevo
>   excidet: ingenio stat sine morte decus.   10

   Is Propertius copying Horace's basic idea? Is Shakespeare (seemingly) influenced by Propertius?

3   Which 'boasts' would you group together? Are there any
    particularly striking similarities, verbal and otherwise, in
    these passages?

4   Whose verse is the most powerful in these extracts?
    Illustrate your answer.

5   Has the convention of such literary claims to immortality
    disappeared? If so, can you suggest a reason why? If not,
    give a modern example.

Propempticon

Ohe, iam satis est, ohe, libelle,
iam pervenimus usque ad umbilicos.
tu procedere adhuc et ire quaeris,
nec summa potes in schida teneri,
sic tamquam tibi res peracta non sit,
quae prima quoque pagina peracta est.
iam lector queriturque deficitque,
iam librarius hoc et ipse dicit
'ohe, iam satis est, ohe, libelle.'

Martial IV. 89

GLOSSARY OF TECHNICAL
TERMS USED IN THE EXERCISES

Alliteration – the beginning with the same letter of two or more words in close connection.

Anaphora – the repetition of a word or phrase in several successive clauses.

Antithesis – such choice or arrangement of words as emphasises a contrast.

Apostrophe – in which the speaker interrupts the thread of the discourse to address pointedly some person present, or supposed to be present.

Assonance – similarity of vowel sounds of words in close juxtaposition.

Asyndeton – in which words or clauses usually connected by conjunctions are left unconnected.

Chiasmus – in which the terms of the second of two parallel phrases reverse the order of the first.

Clausula – the closing words of a period (*q.v.*).

Enjambement – where a verse is not end-stopped, but (to complete its sense) for variety or for effect flows over into the next verse before a pause is reached.

Hyperbole – an exaggerated or extravagant statement, used to express strong feeling.

Imagery – any vivid, descriptive language: usually taken in its limited sense to mean metaphors and similes.

Irony – conveying the real meaning by saying the opposite.

Metaphor – condensed simile (*q.v.*), but with the words of comparing omitted.

Onomatopoeia – where a word's sound resembles what it signifies; or, by extension, a sentence or phrase so formed.

Paradox – an apparent contradiction of facts, by which the real truth is made all the more surprising.

Period – generally taken to mean a complete sentence consisting of several members – especially a well-formed, harmonious sentence. Prose of such a nature is 'periodic prose'.

Peroration – the close of a speech, often taking the form of a summary.

Personification – the attribution of life and consequent actions to inanimate objects or abstract ideas.

Phoneme – a class of similar sounds significantly different from others. Phonemes are the smallest units that go to make up a sound system (see nos. 9 and 17).

Pun – a play on words of similar sound but different meaning, or, by extension, a play on two different meanings of the same word.

Rhetorical question – a form of question used for emphasis and effect, but not requiring an actual answer.

Simile – introduction of an object, scene or action by way of comparison for explanatory, illustrative or ornamental purpose.

Symmetry – the balance of words, phrases, clauses of equal weight within the period. Used sometimes of periods within the paragraph or section.

Tricolon – three cola, or members – a popular structure in Classical literature, in both verse and prose; often with 'increasing members', sometimes with 'decreasing members', according to the desired effect. (A *tetracolon* structure is also common: this tends to fall into balanced halves.)

A SHORT BIBLIOGRAPHY

Some critical works which are recommended reading for the Classical student:

A. GENERAL

D. Daiches, *Critical Approaches to Literature* (Longmans 1956).

R. Fowler (ed.), *Essays on Style and Language* (R. & K.P. 1966).

G. N. Leech, *A Linguistic Guide to English Poetry* (Longmans 1969).

F. L. Lucas, *Style* (Cassell & Co. Ltd 1955; Pan 1964).

J. Reeves, *The Critical Sense* (Heinemann 1956).

I. A. Richards, *Practical Criticism* (R. & K.P. 1929).
  Principles of Literary Criticism (R. & K.P. 1926).

T. Sebeok (ed.), *Style in Language* (MIT Technology Press, N.Y. Wiley 1960).

G. Steiner, *The Language Animal* (in *Encounter* Sept. 1969).

D. Thompson, *Reading and Discrimination* (Chatto & Windus 1957).

B. L. Whorf, *Language, Thought and Reality* (MIT Technology Press, N.Y. Wiley 1956).

B. GENERAL CLASSICAL

J. D. Denniston, *Greek Prose Style* (OUP 1952).

P. Green, *Essays in Antiquity* (nos. 1 & 9) (John Murray 1960).

G. Highet, *Poets in a Landscape* (Hamish Hamilton 1957).

R. A. Hornsby, *Reading Latin Poetry* (Univ. of Oklahoma Press 1967).

K. Quinn, *Latin Explorations* (R. & K.P. 1963).

L. P. Wilkinson, *Golden Latin Artistry* (CUP 1966).

G. Williams, *Tradition and Originality in Roman Poetry* (OUP 1968).

C. SPECIAL AUTHORS

I. CATULLUS

K. Quinn, *The Catullan Revolution* (Melbourne UP 1959).
In *Critical Essays on Roman Literature*, vol. I. *Elegy and Lyric*, 31–63 (R. & K.P. 1962).

II. HOMER

G. Steiner & R. Fagles (ed.), *Homer: A Collection of Critical Essays* (Prentice-Hall Inc. 1962).

III. HORACE

Steele Commager, *The Odes of Horace* (Yale UP 1962).
E. Fraenkel, *Horace* (OUP 1957).
R. G. M. Nisbet, in *Critical Essays on Roman Literature* vol. I, 181–218 (R. & K.P. 1962).
R. G. M. Nisbet & Margaret Hubbard, *A Commentary on Horace Odes Bk. 1* (OUP 1970).
Niall Rudd, *The Satires of Horace* (CUP 1966).
D. West, *Reading Horace* (Edinburgh UP 1967).
L. P. Wilkinson, *Horace and his Lyric Poetry* (CUP 1946).
G. Williams, *The Third Book of Horace's Odes* (OUP 1969).

IV. JUVENAL

G. Highet, *Juvenal the Satirist* (OUP 1954).

V. LUCRETIUS

D. West, *The Images and Poetry of Lucretius* (Edin. UP 1969).

VI. OVID

L. P. Wilkinson, *Ovid Recalled* (CUP 1955).

VII. VIRGIL

Brooks Otis, *Virgil. A Study in Civilized Poetry* (OUP 1963).
V. Pöschl, *The Art of Virgil* (tr. by Gerda Seligson) (Ann Arbor, Michigan, 1962).
M. C. Putnam, *The Poetry of the Aeneid* (OUP 1965).
K. Quinn, *The Aeneid: a critical description* (R. & K.P. 1968).
L. P. Wilkinson, *The Georgics. A Critical Survey* (CUP 1969).

D. SCHOOL BOOKS

M. G. Balme and M. S. Warman, *Aestimanda* (OUP 1965).
D. G. Fratter, *Aere Perennius* (Macmillan 1968).

INDEX OF PASSAGES